365 Days Before His Throne: A Worshipper's Daily Declarations

Draw Near. Bow Low. Rise in His Glory

Gerard Assey

365 Days Before His Throne:
A Worshipper's Daily Declarations
Draw Near. Bow Low. Rise in His Glory
By
Gerard Assey

Published by:
Gerard Assey
19/18, Palli Arasan Street
Anna Nagar East
Chennai - 600 102

ISBN: 978-81-995001-1-2

Table of Contents

Preface

Worship is not a moment. It is not confined to melodies, music, or Sunday gatherings. Worship is the very breath and rhythm of a heart that recognizes the majesty of the King. It is the soul's continual bowing before the glory of the One who was, and is, and is to come.

This book, '**365 Days Before His Throne: *A Worshipper's Daily Declarations***- *(Draw Near. Bow Low. Rise in His Glory)'* was birthed from a deep desire to lead every believer into a daily posture of worship — not through performance, but through *presence*. Each day's declaration is an invitation to draw near, to bow low in humility, and to rise in His glory and strength.

Every word written here is more than a devotion; it is a call to encounter. It invites you to stand where heaven and earth meet — before His throne — in awe, surrender, and adoration. These 365 declarations are meant to renew your mind, align your heart, and recalibrate your spirit to the heartbeat of Heaven.

May each day's reflection draw you deeper into intimacy with the Father, the Son, and the Holy Spirit. May your worship transcend words, filling your atmosphere with His tangible presence. And as you journey through this year of declarations, may you find yourself transformed — from a singer of songs to a carrier of His glory.

Draw near. Bow low. Rise in His glory.
You are invited to live *before His throne* — every day of your life.

How to Use This Book

To experience the fullness of these worship declarations, this book is designed to be a *daily companion*, guiding you through a 365-day journey of adoration and transformation.
Here's how you can best use it:

1. Choose a Consistent Time

- ✓ Set apart a *sacred moment* every day.
- ✓ Early morning is ideal — before the noise of the day begins — so your heart starts aligned with heaven.
- ✓ Or at night — as an offering of reflection and gratitude before resting in His presence.
- ✓ Consistency will cultivate intimacy. Treat it as a daily appointment *before His throne.*

2. Prepare Your Atmosphere

- ✓ Create a worship space — quiet, uncluttered, and inviting.
- ✓ Light a candle, play gentle worship music, or simply sit in silence.
- ✓ Keep your Bible, a journal, and a pen nearby to record what the Holy Spirit speaks.

3. Read, Reflect, and Declare

- ✓ Begin by reading the scripture for the day slowly and reverently.
- ✓ Meditate on the short reflection, allowing the Spirit to personalize it to your heart.
- ✓ Speak the declaration out loud with faith and authority — let it rise like incense before the Lord.
- ✓ Remember: *Worship is both spoken and lived.*

4. **Journal Your Encounters**
   - ✓ After each devotion, write what you sensed, heard, or experienced.
   - ✓ These become your *personal altars of remembrance* — evidence of your growing intimacy with God.
   - ✓ Over time, you will see patterns of divine transformation.
5. **Integrate Worship Throughout the Day**
   - ✓ Don't leave your worship in your morning devotion.
   - ✓ Carry its essence into your work, relationships, and conversations.
   - ✓ Whisper short declarations during the day — "*Lord, I exalt You here,*" or "*You are worthy in this place.*"
   - ✓ This keeps your spirit tuned to His presence continually.
6. **Use It Personally or Collectively**
   - ✓ Personally: as your daily devotional journey before the Lord.
   - ✓ In groups: use it in worship teams, prayer meetings, or church gatherings as a daily or weekly reflection.
   - ✓ Each declaration can spark deeper worship encounters corporately.
7. **At Year's End — Reflect on the Journey**
   - ✓ After completing all 365 days, return to your journal.
   - ✓ Notice how your perspective, language, and intimacy with God have changed. You'll realize — you haven't just read a book; you've *walked with the King.*

Final Encouragement:

This is not a book to be rushed but to be *soaked in.* Let each day's word linger in your spirit. Allow the Holy Spirit to turn each declaration into a *living experience* before His throne.

As you journey through this year of worship, may your life become a continuous offering of praise — a testimony that the presence of God is not just to be visited, but *inhabited.*

Month 1
Days 1–31

Day 1 – The Call to Worship

Scripture: *"Oh come, let us worship and bow down; let us kneel before the Lord our Maker."* — Psalm 95:6

Revelation:

Worship is an invitation, not a demand. God calls us to come near—to bow, to kneel, to yield. It's not about our performance but about His presence. Every act of surrender is an act of worship.

Declaration:

Today I come willingly before my Maker. I bow my heart and lift my voice in love and reverence to Him alone.

Day 2 – Spirit and Truth

Scripture: *"God is Spirit, and those who worship Him must worship in spirit and truth."* — John 4:24

Revelation:

True worship transcends words and rituals. It flows from a heart aligned with truth. When our spirit connects with His, heaven meets earth in holy communion.

Declaration:

I worship You, Lord, in spirit and in truth. Let my heart always mirror Your truth as I adore You.

Day 3 – The Beauty of Holiness

Scripture: *"Give unto the Lord the glory due His name; worship the Lord in the beauty of holiness."* — Psalm 29:2

Revelation:
Holiness beautifies worship. It's not perfection, but purity of devotion—when the heart is uncluttered by idols and distractions. God delights in a heart set apart for Him.
Declaration:
Lord, let my worship reflect the beauty of Your holiness. Cleanse my heart and fill it with the light of Your glory.

Day 4 – A Living Sacrifice

Scripture: *"Present your bodies a living sacrifice, holy, acceptable to God, which is your reasonable service."* — Romans 12:1
Revelation:
Worship is not confined to songs; it's the offering of one's entire being. Every thought, word, and action can rise as worship when yielded to Him.
Declaration:
Lord, I offer my life to You today—my mind, my hands, my heart—as a living act of worship.

Day 5 – The Power of Praise

Scripture: *"Let everything that has breath praise the Lord."* — Psalm 150:6
Revelation:
Praise is the sound of life. Every breath carries the potential to glorify God. When creation praises, it testifies to His greatness.
Declaration:
With every breath I have, I will praise You, Lord! My life will echo Your glory.

Day 6 – The Altar of the Heart

Scripture: *"But the hour is coming, and now is, when the true worshipers will worship the Father in spirit and truth."* — John 4:23

Revelation:

The altar of worship is no longer made of stone—it's the human heart. God seeks worshippers, not performances. He looks for hearts that are sincere and yielded.

Declaration:

Father, let my heart be Your altar. May pure worship rise continually before You.

Day 7 – Worship in the Storm

Scripture: *"At midnight Paul and Silas were praying and singing hymns to God."* — Acts 16:25

Revelation:

Worship in adversity is the highest form of faith. It declares that God is still good even when circumstances aren't. Heaven opens where praise defies pain.

Declaration:

Even in my storms, I will sing. My worship will rise above my trials and touch heaven.

Day 8 – The Song of the Redeemed

Scripture: *"They sang a new song, saying: 'You are worthy… for You were slain, and have redeemed us to God by Your blood.'"* — Revelation 5:9

Revelation:

Only the redeemed can truly sing the song of redemption. Worship remembers the Cross and celebrates freedom. Gratitude is the melody of the redeemed.

Declaration:

Thank You, Jesus, for redeeming me. My song belongs to You alone.

Day 9 – Bow Before Majesty

Scripture: *"Come, let us bow down in worship, let us kneel before the Lord our Maker."* — Psalm 95:6

Revelation:

Bowing is the physical expression of spiritual humility. It's a declaration that He reigns supreme and we are His. The lowlier we bow, the higher He is lifted.

Declaration:

Lord, I bow before Your majesty. You are enthroned above all, and I worship You.

Day 10 – The Fragrance of Worship

Scripture: *"Mary took a pound of costly perfume… and anointed Jesus' feet, and the house was filled with the fragrance."* — John 12:3

Revelation:

Worship leaves a fragrance that fills the atmosphere. True adoration costs something—it pours out love without restraint.

Declaration:

Lord, let my worship today be like a sweet fragrance before You, poured out in love.

Day 11 – Worship and Wonder

Scripture: *"Let all the earth fear the Lord; let all the inhabitants of the world stand in awe of Him."* — Psalm 33:8

Revelation:

Worship begins where words end—in wonder. The more we behold His greatness, the smaller everything else becomes.

Declaration:
I stand in awe of You, Lord. Your majesty leaves me speechless and my heart full.

Day 12 – Singing from the Heart

Scripture: *"Sing and make music in your heart to the Lord."* — Ephesians 5:19
Revelation:
Songs that rise from the heart reach the heart of God. Worship is not performance—it's communion.
Declaration:
Lord, I sing to You from the depths of my heart. May every note glorify You.

Day 13 – Worship Through Obedience

Scripture: *"To obey is better than sacrifice."* — 1 Samuel 15:22
Revelation:
Obedience is the purest form of worship. It proves love in action and devotion in decision.
Declaration:
Father, may my obedience today be my worship. I choose Your will above my own.

Day 14 – The Posture of Gratitude

Scripture: *"Enter His gates with thanksgiving and His courts with praise."* — Psalm 100:4
Revelation:
Gratitude opens the door to worship. A thankful heart recognizes God's hand in all things.
Declaration:
I come before You with thanksgiving, Lord. My heart rejoices in Your goodness and grace.

Day 15 – The Audience of One

Scripture: *"And your Father who sees in secret will reward you."* — Matthew 6:6

Revelation:

Worship is for an audience of One. It's not about who hears us but the One who sees us. Hidden worship is heaven's treasure.

Declaration:

Lord, I worship You alone—seen or unseen. You are my only audience.

Day 16 – Worship in Weakness

Scripture: *"My grace is sufficient for you, for My strength is made perfect in weakness."* — 2 Corinthians 12:9

Revelation:

Our weakness becomes a stage for His glory. Worship in weakness declares His sufficiency.

Declaration:

In my weakness, I worship You, Lord. Your strength is my song and my joy.

Day 17 – The Throne of Grace

Scripture: *"Let us then approach God's throne of grace with confidence."* — Hebrews 4:16

Revelation:

Worship grants us access to the throne room. Grace opens the way, and love keeps us there.

Declaration:

Lord, I approach Your throne with reverence and confidence. I worship You, my King of grace.

Day 18 – Worship in Unity

Scripture: *"Oh, magnify the Lord with me, and let us exalt His name together."* — Psalm 34:3

Revelation:
Worship multiplies in unity. When hearts align in adoration, heaven invades gatherings.
Declaration:
Together, we lift Your name high, Lord. Let our united worship draw Your glory down.

Day 19 – Worship and the Word

Scripture: *"Your word is a lamp to my feet and a light to my path."* — Psalm 119:105
Revelation:
The Word fuels worship. Revelation births adoration. The more we know Him, the deeper we worship.
Declaration:
Your Word lights my heart, Lord. I worship You for who You have revealed Yourself to be.

Day 20 – Worship that Costs

Scripture: *"I will not offer to the Lord that which costs me nothing."* — 2 Samuel 24:24
Revelation:
True worship demands a price—time, pride, comfort. Sacrifice turns ordinary praise into holy offering.
Declaration:
Lord, I give You my best today. My worship will cost me something, for You are worthy of all.

Day 21 – Clothed with Praise

Scripture: *"Put on the garment of praise for the spirit of heaviness."* — Isaiah 61:3
Revelation:
Praise shifts atmospheres. It replaces heaviness with hope and sorrow with song.
Declaration:

I put on praise today. My spirit will rejoice in You, Lord, regardless of circumstance.

Day 22 – Worship in the Waiting

Scripture: *"Rest in the Lord, and wait patiently for Him."* — Psalm 37:7

Revelation:

Waiting is worship when done in trust. It shows faith in God's timing more than our own.

Declaration:

I wait in worship, Lord. My heart rests in the assurance that You are working.

Day 23 – The King is Worthy

Scripture: *"Worthy is the Lamb who was slain."* — Revelation 5:12

Revelation:

All of heaven declares His worth. Worship is the language of eternity. Every crown laid down proclaims: *He alone is worthy.*

Declaration:

Jesus, You are worthy of all glory, honor, and praise. My heart joins heaven's song today.

Day 24 – Worship in Spirit Freedom

Scripture: *"Where the Spirit of the Lord is, there is liberty."* — 2 Corinthians 3:17

Revelation:

The Spirit releases freedom in worship. No chains can survive where His presence dwells.

Declaration:

Spirit of God, move freely in me. Let my worship overflow in holy liberty.

Day 25 – Worship and the Presence

Scripture: *"In Your presence is fullness of joy."* — Psalm 16:11

Revelation:

Worship ushers us into His presence, where joy reigns and peace abides. Every encounter transforms us.

Declaration:

Lord, I seek Your presence above all. In You, I find my joy and my home.

Day 26 – Worship in the Morning

Scripture: *"My voice You shall hear in the morning, O Lord."* — Psalm 5:3

Revelation:

Morning worship sets the tone for the day. When the first voice we hear is His, peace follows.

Declaration:

Lord, I lift my voice to You this morning. You are my first thought and my highest praise.

Day 27 – Worship Through Giving

Scripture: *"Honor the Lord with your wealth and with the firstfruits of all your increase."* — Proverbs 3:9

Revelation:

Giving is worship when done from a joyful heart. It declares that all we have belongs to Him.

Declaration:

Lord, I worship You with my substance. You are my source and my sufficiency.

Day 28 – The Joy of Worship

Scripture: *"Serve the Lord with gladness; come before His presence with singing."* — Psalm 100:2

Revelation:

Worship is joy expressed. Singing is not obligation—it's overflow. Glad hearts make glad worship.

Declaration:

I serve You with gladness, Lord. My song is a celebration of Your goodness.

Day 29 – Worship Through Surrender

Scripture: *"Not my will, but Yours be done."* — Luke 22:42

Revelation:

Surrender is the soul of worship. It's yielding our will to His, trusting His plan above our preference.

Declaration:

Lord, I surrender afresh today. Have Your way in me and through me.

Day 30 – Worship that Transforms

Scripture: *"We all, beholding the glory of the Lord, are being transformed into the same image."* — 2 Corinthians 3:18

Revelation:

Worship changes us. As we behold Him, we become like Him. Transformation is the fruit of true adoration.

Declaration:

As I behold You, Lord, make me more like You. Let my worship shape me into Your likeness.

Day 31 – Worship Forever

Scripture: *"From the rising of the sun to its going down, the Lord's name is to be praised."* — Psalm 113:3

Revelation:

Worship is eternal—it never ceases. The rhythm of heaven is continual praise.

Declaration:

From dawn to dusk, I will bless Your name. My worship will never end, Lord of all.

Month 2
Days 32–59

Day 32 – The Heart That Longs

Scripture: *"As the deer pants for streams of water, so my soul pants for You, O God."* — Psalm 42:1

Revelation:

Worship springs from longing—a soul thirsting for the presence of God. The true worshipper doesn't seek blessings, but the Blesser Himself.

Declaration:

Lord, my soul longs for You. You are my desire, my song, and my satisfaction.

Day 33 – Worship and Fear of the Lord

Scripture: *"Serve the Lord with fear, and rejoice with trembling."* — Psalm 2:11

Revelation:

Reverence and joy coexist in worship. Holy fear keeps our adoration pure and our approach humble.

Declaration:

I worship You, Lord, with reverent joy. You are holy, mighty, and greatly to be feared in all the earth.

Day 34 – Worship in the Secret Place

Scripture: *"He who dwells in the secret place of the Most High shall abide under the shadow of the Almighty."* — Psalm 91:1

Revelation:

The truest worship happens unseen. In the quiet corners of devotion, heaven listens closely.

Declaration:

Lord, meet me in the secret place. Let my hidden worship be a fragrance that pleases You.

Day 35 – The Heart of Thanksgiving

Scripture: *"Give thanks to the Lord, for He is good; His love endures forever."* — Psalm 136:1

Revelation:

Thanksgiving is the gateway to worship. Grateful hearts ignite the fire of adoration.

Declaration:

Thank You, Lord, for Your unfailing love. My heart overflows with gratitude and praise.

Day 36 – Worship and Faith

Scripture: *"Without faith it is impossible to please Him."* — Hebrews 11:6

Revelation:

Worship is an act of faith. We lift our hands not because we see everything clearly, but because we trust the One who reigns.

Declaration:

I worship You, Lord, in faith. Even when I cannot see, I know You are worthy.

Day 37 – The Eternal Song

Scripture: *"Day and night they never cease to say: 'Holy, holy, holy is the Lord God Almighty.'"* — Revelation 4:8

Revelation:

Heaven's atmosphere is worship. The song of holiness never ends—it's the rhythm of eternity.

Declaration:

Holy, holy, holy are You, Lord! I join heaven's song in declaring Your unending greatness.

Day 38 – Worship and Humility

Scripture: *"Humble yourselves before the Lord, and He will lift you up."* — James 4:10

Revelation:

Pride cannot coexist with worship. Humility bows before majesty and finds grace in the lowering.

Declaration:

Lord, I humble myself before You. Lift me only to lift You higher.

Day 39 – Worship Through Tears

Scripture: *"Those who sow in tears shall reap in joy."* — Psalm 126:5

Revelation:

Tears can be worship when offered to God. Sorrow laid at His feet becomes sacred surrender.

Declaration:

Even in my tears, I worship You, Lord. You turn my mourning into melody.

Day 40 – The Silence of Worship

Scripture: *"Be still, and know that I am God."* — Psalm 46:10

Revelation:

Silence can be worship when filled with awe. Stillness says, "You are God, and that is enough."

Declaration:

In stillness I adore You, Lord. My quiet heart resounds with Your greatness.

Day 41 – The Fire of Worship

Scripture: *"The fire on the altar shall be kept burning; it shall never go out."* — Leviticus 6:13

Revelation:

Worship must be tended like fire—daily, intentionally.

The flame of devotion burns brightest when continually fed.

Declaration:

Lord, keep the fire of worship burning in me. Let no distraction dim its glow.

Day 42 – Worship and the Cross

Scripture: *"Far be it from me to boast except in the cross of our Lord Jesus Christ."* — Galatians 6:14

Revelation:

The Cross is the centerpiece of worship. It reveals the cost of love and the depth of grace.

Declaration:

Jesus, I worship You for the Cross. Your sacrifice compels my praise forever.

Day 43 – Worship in Community

Scripture: *"For where two or three are gathered in My name, I am there in the midst of them."* — Matthew 18:20

Revelation:

Corporate worship magnifies presence. Unity draws glory. God delights in collective hearts lifting one voice.

Declaration:

Lord, let our united worship host Your presence. We exalt You together as one body.

Day 44 – The Joyful Sound

Scripture: *"Blessed are the people who know the joyful sound!"* — Psalm 89:15

Revelation:

The sound of worship brings blessing. Joyful praise shifts atmospheres and awakens faith.

Declaration:

Lord, fill my heart with the sound of joy. Let my worship echo Your gladness.

Day 45 – Worship Through Trials

Scripture: *"Though He slay me, yet will I trust Him."* — Job 13:15

Revelation:

Unshaken worship proves trust. Faithful hearts sing even when broken. Worship becomes warfare in pain.

Declaration:

Even in my trials, I will worship You. My trust will never waver, my praise will not cease.

Day 46 – Worship on Holy Ground

Scripture: *"Take your sandals off your feet, for the place where you stand is holy ground."* — Exodus 3:5

Revelation:

God's presence sanctifies ordinary spaces. When He shows up, every ground becomes holy.

Declaration:

Lord, I recognize Your presence here. My heart bows in reverence on holy ground.

Day 47 – The Dance of Worship

Scripture: *"Let them praise His name with dancing."* — Psalm 149:3

Revelation:

Worship involves the whole being. When the heart rejoices, even the feet express praise.

Declaration:

Lord, my whole body will praise You. My movement declares Your freedom and joy.

Day 48 – Worship and the Nations

Scripture: *"All the nations You have made shall come and worship before You, O Lord."* — Psalm 86:9

Revelation:

Worship unites the nations under one King. Every language and culture finds its truest voice before the throne.

Declaration:

Lord, let the nations worship You! May my life be part of the global chorus declaring Your glory.

Day 49 – Worship that Breaks Chains

Scripture: *"Suddenly there was a great earthquake… and everyone's chains were loosed."* — Acts 16:26

Revelation:

Worship shakes prisons and looses captives. Praise opens doors no key can.

Declaration:

My worship has power! As I lift my voice, chains fall and freedom reigns in Jesus' name.

Day 50 – The Shepherd's Worshipper

Scripture: *"The Lord is my shepherd; I shall not want."* — Psalm 23:1

Revelation:

Worship flows from trust in the Shepherd's care. Knowing He provides silences fear and stirs adoration.

Declaration:

Lord, You are my Shepherd. I worship You for Your goodness and faithfulness to me.

Day 51 – Worship Through Waiting on His Voice

Scripture: *"Speak, Lord, for Your servant is listening."* — 1 Samuel 3:10

Revelation:

Listening is part of worship. The heart that pauses to hear God honors Him most deeply.

Declaration:

Lord, I quiet my heart to hear You. Your voice is my worship's reward.

Day 52 – Worship and the Glory Cloud

Scripture: *"The glory of the Lord filled the house of the Lord."* — 1 Kings 8:11

Revelation:

When worship rises, glory descends. God inhabits the praises of His people and fills the atmosphere with His presence.

Declaration:

Fill this place, Lord, with Your glory. Let my worship invite Your holy presence to dwell.

Day 53 – Worship Beyond Words

Scripture: *"For we do not know what to pray as we ought, but the Spirit Himself intercedes for us."* — Romans 8:26

Revelation:

Sometimes worship transcends language. When words fail, the Spirit sings within.

Declaration:

Holy Spirit, sing through me. Let my wordless worship touch the heart of the Father.

Day 54 – Worship and the King's Beauty

Scripture: *"Gaze upon the beauty of the Lord and seek Him in His temple."* — Psalm 27:4

Revelation:

Worship is beholding beauty—the beauty of holiness, mercy, and majesty. The more we gaze, the more we're transformed.

Declaration:

Lord, I behold Your beauty today. You are fairer than all, and my heart is captivated by You.

Day 55 – The Overflow of Worship

Scripture: *"Out of the abundance of the heart the mouth speaks."* — Matthew 12:34

Revelation:

Worship overflows naturally from a full heart. The more we commune with Him, the more praise spills out.

Declaration:

My heart overflows with love for You, Lord. My lips cannot contain the praise You deserve.

Day 56 – Worship in the Night

Scripture: *"At midnight I will rise to give thanks to You."* — Psalm 119:62

Revelation:

Worship doesn't depend on time. Even in the darkest hours, praise keeps the light burning.

Declaration:

Lord, even in the night, I will thank You. My praise will pierce the darkness.

Day 57 – Worship and Holiness of Heart

Scripture: *"Blessed are the pure in heart, for they shall see God."* — Matthew 5:8

Revelation:
Purity prepares the heart for true worship. Sin clouds vision, but holiness restores sight.
Declaration:
Lord, purify my heart that I may see You clearly and worship You fully.

Day 58 – The Strength of Worship

Scripture: *"The joy of the Lord is your strength."* — Nehemiah 8:10
Revelation:
Joy in worship strengthens the soul. Praising God recharges weary hearts with divine energy.
Declaration:
Lord, Your joy is my strength! I worship You with gladness and courage renewed.

Day 59 – Worship that Invites Heaven

Scripture: *"Your kingdom come, Your will be done on earth as it is in heaven."* — Matthew 6:10
Revelation:
Worship brings heaven to earth. Each song of adoration aligns earth's sound with heaven's reality.
Declaration:
Let my worship today echo heaven's sound, Lord. May Your kingdom come through my praise.

Month 3
Days 60–90

Day 60 – The Majesty of His Name

Scripture: *"Your name, O Lord, endures for ever, your renown, O Lord, through all generations."* — Psalm 135:13

Revelation:

Worship acknowledges the enduring nature of God's name—unchanged, unshakeable, forever worthy. When we lift His name, we recognise the eternal character of God.

Declaration:

I worship Your name, Lord—an everlasting name. You are the same yesterday, today and forever.

Day 61 – Worship in the Wilderness

Scripture: *"My soul thirsts for God, for the living God. When shall I come and appear before God?"* — Psalm 42:2

Revelation:

Worship rises even in the dry places. The longing of the soul in the wilderness becomes worship when directed toward the living God.

Declaration:

In this season of thirst, I worship You, Lord. You are living water; I draw near.

Day 62 – The Anchor of Worship

Scripture: *"He who dwells in the shelter of the Most High will rest in the shadow of the Almighty."* — Psalm 91:1

Revelation:

Worship finds its refuge under His shadow—peace

and strength wrapped in His presence. Adoration becomes our shelter.

Declaration:

Lord, I find rest in worshiping You. In Your shadow I am safe, secure and satisfied.

Day 63 – Worship and the Word Within

Scripture: *"Let the word of Christ dwell in you richly… with gratitude in your hearts to God."* — Colossians 3:16

Revelation:

Worship is nourished by God's Word planted in our hearts. The Word becomes the wellspring of praise and gratitude.

Declaration:

Holy Word, dwell richly in me. Let my worship overflow from the truth You have planted.

Day 64 – Worship Beyond the Mountain Top

Scripture: *"And he said, 'My presence will go with you, and I will give you rest.'"* — Exodus 33:14

Revelation:

Worship isn't only when the mountain trembles—it's when He goes with us through the valleys too. Presence is the heart of worship.

Declaration:

You go before me, Lord. My worship travels with You; I rest in Your faithful presence.

Day 65 – The Silence That Hears

Scripture: *"Be still and know that I am God."* — Psalm 46:10

Revelation:

Sometimes worship is silent. In quiet surrender we let

Him speak and we simply adore.
Declaration:
In stillness I acknowledge You, Lord. My worship is a quiet heart bowed in reverence.

Day 66 – Worship in His Greatness

Scripture: *"Great is the Lord and most worthy of praise; his greatness no one can fathom."* — Psalm 145:3
Revelation:
Worship is recognising the vastness of God's greatness. Our finite words fall short, yet our hearts respond with awe.
Declaration:
Lord, You are infinitely great. I worship You with awe and wonder.

Day 67 – The Freedom of Worship

Scripture: *"Now the Lord is the Spirit, and where the Spirit of the Lord is, there is freedom."* — 2 Corinthians 3:17
Revelation:
Worship frees us. In His presence chains drop, walls crumble, and the heart dances with liberty.
Declaration:
I worship You in freedom, Spirit of the Lord. Your presence releases my heart.

Day 68 – Worship From a Thankful Heart

Scripture: *"I will praise You, Lord, among the nations; I will sing of You among the peoples."* — Psalm 108:3
Revelation:
Worship from thanksgiving goes beyond self—it reaches nations, declares glory, honours God

publicly and privately.

Declaration:

Thank You, Lord, for Your works among the nations. My worship rises from a grateful heart.

Day 69 – Worship in His Discipline

Scripture: *"Those whom I love I rebuke and discipline. So be earnest and repent."* — Revelation 3:19

Revelation:

Even discipline can become worship when we embrace it as part of God's loving correction. Our response is adoration, not resentment.

Declaration:

Lord, I honour Your discipline. My worship rises in obedience and trust in Your good hand.

Day 70 – Worship in the Heavens

Scripture: *"Praise the Lord in his sanctuary; praise him in his mighty heavens."* — Psalm 150:1

Revelation:

Our worship aligns with heaven's chorus. Earth and heaven merge as we adore.

Declaration:

My worship joins the heavens, Lord. I lift Your name in the sanctuary of Your presence.

Day 71 – The Heart Set Apart

Scripture: *"You are a chosen people, a royal priesthood… that you may declare the praises of him who called you out of darkness."* — 1 Peter 2:9

Revelation:

Worship flows from identity—we are called out of darkness to praise. Our priestly role is to declare His worth.

Declaration:
Lord, I declare Your praises. You've called me into the light, and I worship You.

Day 72 – Worship With Perseverance

Scripture: *"By perseverance the righteous will inherit the land."* — Hebrews 10:36
Revelation:
Worship perseveres when the journey is long. Holding fast to praise becomes our strength.
Declaration:
I worship You, Lord, with steadfast devotion. My praise does not waver.

Day 73 – Worship and the Covenant Love

Scripture: *"For the Lord is good and his love endures forever; his faithfulness continues through all generations."* — Psalm 100:5
Revelation:
Worship celebrates covenant love—God's unending faithfulness across time. We join generations in adoration.
Declaration:
Your love endures forever, Lord. I worship You for Your faithfulness through all generations.

Day 74 – Worship in Everyday Life

Scripture: *"So whether you eat or drink or whatever you do, do it all for the glory of God."* — 1 Corinthians 10:31
Revelation:
Worship isn't confined to sanctuary walls—it permeates every action, every moment. Life becomes the offering.
Declaration:

Today I worship You in every detail—my words, my business, my choices—all for Your glory.

Day 75 – Worship That Invites His Name

Scripture: *"At the name of Jesus every knee should bow… and every tongue confess that Jesus Christ is Lord."* — Philippians 2:10–11

Revelation:

Worship under His name invites response. Every knee will bow and every tongue confess—our worship participates in that proclamation.

Declaration:

Jesus, at Your name I bow. My worship adds to the chorus of heaven declaring You Lord.

Day 76 – Worship From Our Whole Being

Scripture: *"Let everything that has breath praise the Lord."* — Psalm 150:6

Revelation:

Worship engages all creation. Every breath, every beat of our being is designed to praise.

Declaration:

With every breath I take, I worship You, Lord. My life becomes an offering of praise.

Day 77 – Worship in the Waiting Season

Scripture: *"But as for me, I will look to the Lord; I will wait for the God of my salvation."* — Micah 7:7

Revelation:

Waiting becomes worship when I fix my eyes on the God of salvation. Patience is devotion in slow motion.

Declaration:

In the time of waiting, I worship You. My hope rests in You alone.

Day 78 – Worship and Resurrection Life

Scripture: *"God raised us up with Christ and seated us with him in the heavenly realms."* — Ephesians 2:6

Revelation:

Worship acknowledges our new identity—alive in Him, seated in heavenly realms. Our worship springs from resurrection life.

Declaration:

Lord, I worship You from the realms of resurrection. I am alive in You and my praise rises accordingly.

Day 79 – Worship of the Saviour

Scripture: *"When they saw the star, they were overjoyed. On coming to the house, they saw the child… They worshiped him."* — Matthew 2:10–11

Revelation:

The wise men set aside everything to worship at the sight of Jesus. True worship forsakes distraction and draws near.

Declaration:

Jesus, I worship You as my Saviour. My heart follows You wherever You lead.

Day 80 – Worship With Boldness

Scripture: *"Let us then approach God's throne of grace with confidence."* — Hebrews 4:16

Revelation:

Worship enters boldly into the throne room—not on the basis of merit but by grace. Boldness becomes worship's posture.

Declaration:

With confidence I draw near, Lord. My worship stands before Your throne by Your grace.

Day 81 – Worship of the Living God

Scripture: *"You are my God, I will give thanks to you; you are my God, I will exalt you."* — Psalm 118:28

Revelation:

Worship is personal—"You are my God." It flows from relational knowledge, not distant admiration.

Declaration:

You are my God. I exalt You, I thank You, and I worship You now and forever.

Day 82 – Worship in the Midst of Praise

Scripture: *"And all the congregation of the children of Israel … sang a song unto the Lord, and spoke, saying, 'I will sing unto the Lord, for he hath triumphed gloriously.'"* — Exodus 15:1

Revelation:

Worship is triumphant—after deliverance comes song. The congregation lifts up a melody of victory.

Declaration:

Lord, You have triumphed gloriously. My worship joins the song of victory.

Day 83 – Worship of the Lamb

Scripture: *"Worthy is the Lamb who was slain, to receive power and riches and wisdom and strength and honour and glory and praise!"* — Revelation 5:12

Revelation:

Jesus, the Lamb, is the centre of our worship. His sacrifice reorders our praise and declares His worth.

Declaration:

Worthy is the Lamb! My worship flows to Him who died for me and now reigns forever.

Day 84 – Worship that Bears Fruit

Scripture: *"And let the peace of Christ rule in your hearts… And be thankful."* — Colossians 3:15

Revelation:

Worship cultivates peace and gratitude within. A heart ruled by peace offers fruit in praise.

Declaration:

Peace of Christ, reign in me. My worship produces the fruit of thanksgiving and calm surrender.

Day 85 – Worship and the Hidden Treasure

Scripture: *"For where your treasure is, there your heart will be also."* — Matthew 6:21

Revelation:

Worship reveals where our treasure lies. When the heart treasures God, worship becomes its natural outflow.

Declaration:

Lord, You are my treasure. My heart is fixed on You and my worship aligns with that reality.

Day 86 – Worship of the Creator

Scripture: *"For by him all things were created… and in him all things hold together."* — Colossians 1:16–17

Revelation:

Worship honours the Creator who sustains all things. Recognising His creative power invites our adoration.

Declaration:

Creator of all, I worship You. Everything exists because of You—my praise acknowledges Your hand.

Day 87 – Worship With Hope

Scripture: *"Let us not give up meeting together… but let us encourage one another—and all the more as you see the Day approaching."* — Hebrews 10:25

Revelation:

Worship in fellowship builds hope. Shared adoration becomes anticipation for the day of the Lord.

Declaration:

Together we worship, Lord. Our unity anticipates Your coming and our hope is anchored in You.

Day 88 – Worship in Holiness of Character

Scripture: *"Be holy, because I am holy."* — 1 Peter 1:16

Revelation:

Worship calls us into holy living. Adoration of God transforms our character so we mirror Him.

Declaration:

Lord, I strive for holiness because You are holy. My worship expresses in how I live each day.

Day 89 – Worship in the Midst of Joy

Scripture: *"Make a joyful noise to the Lord, all the earth! Serve the Lord with gladness! Come into his presence with singing!"* — Psalm 100:1–2

Revelation:

Worship erupts from glad hearts. Celebration is an appropriate posture when we come into His presence.

Declaration:

With gladness I serve You, Lord. My worship rises in singing and celebratory praise.

Day 90 – Worship in the Promise of His Return

Scripture: *“He who testifies to these things says, ‘Yes, I am coming soon.’”* — Revelation 22:20

Revelation:

Worship is anchored in the promise of His return. Knowing He is coming strengthens our present adoration.

Declaration:

Amen. Even so, come, Lord Jesus. My worship anticipates Your return and bows in joyful hope.

Month 4
Days 91–120

Day 91 – Worship in Spirit and Truth

Scripture: *"But the hour is coming, and now is, when the true worshippers shall worship the Father in spirit and in truth."* — John 4:23

Revelation:
True worship transcends ritual and form. It flows from the Spirit within us and aligns with the truth of who God is.

Declaration:
Lord, I worship You in spirit and in truth. My heart and my life echo the reality of who You are.

Day 92 – Worship That Pleases the Father

Scripture: *"Therefore, since we are receiving a kingdom that cannot be shaken, let us be thankful, and so worship God acceptably with reverence and awe."* — Hebrews 12:28

Revelation:
Acceptable worship carries reverence and gratitude. Awe is the fragrance that pleases the Father's heart.

Declaration:
I worship You with reverence and gratitude, Lord. My heart trembles joyfully before Your unshakable Kingdom.

Day 93 – Worship that Ascends as Incense

Scripture: *"Let my prayer be set forth before thee as incense; and the lifting up of my hands as the evening sacrifice."* — Psalm 141:2

Revelation:
Worship is incense rising—a sweet aroma before the throne. Every lifted hand and whispered prayer carries fragrance to heaven.
Declaration:
Lord, let my worship rise like incense before You—pure, pleasing, and constant.

Day 94 – Worship in His Holiness

Scripture: *"Exalt the Lord our God and worship at His footstool; He is holy."* — Psalm 99:5
Revelation:
To worship in holiness is to recognise the purity of His being. Holiness draws us into deep reverence and joyful humility.
Declaration:
Holy God, I bow before You. My worship honours Your perfect holiness.

Day 95 – Worship that Builds an Altar

Scripture: *"Then Abram built an altar there to the Lord who had appeared to him."* — Genesis 12:7
Revelation:
Worship builds spiritual altars—places of remembrance where encounters with God become memorials of devotion.
Declaration:
Today I build an altar of worship, Lord. May my heart forever remember Your presence and promises.

Day 96 – Worship Through Obedience

Scripture: *"To obey is better than sacrifice."* — 1 Samuel 15:22
Revelation:
Obedience is worship in motion. Our submission to

God's will becomes a living act of praise.
Declaration:
Lord, I worship You with my obedience. May every step I take honour Your command.

Day 97 – Worship that Draws Fire

Scripture: *"Then fire came out from the presence of the Lord and consumed the burnt offering on the altar."* — Leviticus 9:24
Revelation:
When worship is pure, the fire of His presence falls. Divine response meets human surrender.
Declaration:
Let Your fire fall, Lord! Consume my offering of worship until only Your glory remains.

Day 98 – Worship in Unity

Scripture: *"When the trumpeters and singers were as one… the glory of the Lord filled the house of God."* — 2 Chronicles 5:13–14
Revelation:
Heaven responds to unified worship. When hearts and voices are one, the glory of the Lord fills the atmosphere.
Declaration:
Lord, unite our hearts in worship. Let Your glory fill our gatherings as one sound rises to You.

Day 99 – Worship that Opens Prison Doors

Scripture: *"At midnight Paul and Silas were praying and singing hymns to God… and immediately all the doors were opened."* — Acts 16:25–26
Revelation:
Worship in hardship breaks chains and opens

impossible doors. Praise is power in motion.
Declaration:
Even in the darkest night, I worship You. My song shakes the foundations, for You inhabit my praise.

Day 100 – Worship of the Glorious King

Scripture: *"Lift up your heads, O you gates… and the King of glory shall come in."* — Psalm 24:7
Revelation:
Worship is an open gate inviting the King of Glory to enter. Our adoration welcomes His presence.
Declaration:
King of Glory, come in! My heart's gate is wide open in worship to You.

Day 101 – Worship in Brokenness

Scripture: *"A broken and contrite heart, O God, You will not despise."* — Psalm 51:17
Revelation:
Worship doesn't hide its cracks. God receives the broken heart as a beautiful sacrifice.
Declaration:
Lord, I worship You with honesty and humility. My brokenness becomes my altar before You.

Day 102 – Worship that Confounds the Enemy

Scripture: *"As they began to sing and praise, the Lord set ambushes against their enemies."* — 2 Chronicles 20:22
Revelation:
Worship is warfare. The sound of praise releases divine strategy and victory.
Declaration:

I lift my song of worship, Lord. Let praise scatter every enemy before You.

Day 103 – Worship in the Secret Place

Scripture: *"But when you pray, go into your room, close the door and pray to your Father, who is unseen."* — Matthew 6:6

Revelation:

Private worship builds public strength. The unseen moments with God sustain every outward act.

Declaration:

In the secret place I worship You, Father. My intimacy with You fuels every expression of praise.

Day 104 – Worship and the Fear of the Lord

Scripture: *"Serve the Lord with fear, and rejoice with trembling."* — Psalm 2:11

Revelation:

Reverent worship blends joy with awe. The fear of the Lord purifies our hearts and deepens our praise.

Declaration:

I rejoice with holy fear, Lord. My worship balances delight and reverence before You.

Day 105 – Worship that Costs Something

Scripture: *"I will not offer to the Lord my God that which costs me nothing."* — 2 Samuel 24:24

Revelation:

True worship carries a price—our time, comfort, and pride. Love gives extravagantly to the One who is worthy.

Declaration:

Lord, my worship costs me something, and I offer it freely because You deserve everything.

Day 106 – Worship and His Nearness

Scripture: *"The Lord is near to all who call on Him, to all who call on Him in truth."* — Psalm 145:18

Revelation:

Worship invites nearness. As we call upon Him sincerely, His presence draws close and fills the space.

Declaration:

Lord, I call upon You in truth. Let my worship draw Your nearness like a comforting embrace.

Day 107 – Worship that Magnifies

Scripture: *"Oh, magnify the Lord with me, and let us exalt His name together."* — Psalm 34:3

Revelation:

Worship magnifies—not that God grows larger, but our perception of Him does. Praise expands our view of His greatness.

Declaration:

Together we magnify You, Lord. I exalt Your name above every name and circumstance.

Day 108 – Worship that Renews Strength

Scripture: *"They that wait upon the Lord shall renew their strength."* — Isaiah 40:31

Revelation:

Waiting in worship refreshes the weary soul. As we adore Him, strength rises on wings of trust.

Declaration:

I wait on You in worship, Lord. Renew my strength and lift me higher in Your presence.

Day 109 – Worship in the House of the Lord

Scripture: *"I was glad when they said to me, 'Let us go into the house of the Lord.'"* — Psalm 122:1

Revelation:

Corporate worship brings joy. There's a unique gladness when God's people gather to bless His name.

Declaration:

With gladness I enter Your house, Lord. My heart rejoices in the fellowship of worship.

Day 110 – Worship of the Faithful God

Scripture: *"Your faithfulness reaches to the skies."* — Psalm 36:5

Revelation:

Worship celebrates His faithfulness—immeasurable, unchanging, and dependable through generations.

Declaration:

Faithful God, I worship You. Your constancy anchors my praise forever.

Day 111 – Worship that Restores Joy

Scripture: *"You have turned my mourning into dancing."* — Psalm 30:11

Revelation:

Worship transforms sorrow. When praise begins, joy returns, and heaviness departs.

Declaration:

Lord, I worship You through my tears until You turn them into dancing. You restore my joy.

Day 112 – Worship in the Beauty of Holiness

Scripture: *"Give unto the Lord the glory due unto His name; worship the Lord in the beauty of holiness."* — Psalm 29:2

Revelation:

Holiness beautifies worship. The purity of heart and the splendor of His presence adorn our praise.

Declaration:

Lord, I worship You in the beauty of holiness. Your glory is my delight and my song.

Day 113 – Worship that Waits for His Voice

Scripture: *"Speak, Lord, for Your servant is listening."* — 1 Samuel 3:10

Revelation:

Worship listens. Adoration pauses to hear the whisper of His Spirit and respond in surrender.

Declaration:

Speak, Lord. My worship is attentive, my heart is still, my ears are open to Your voice.

Day 114 – Worship in the Morning

Scripture: *"My voice You shall hear in the morning, O Lord; in the morning I will direct it to You, and I will look up."* — Psalm 5:3

Revelation:

Morning worship sets the tone of the day. The first words we speak shape our focus toward God.

Declaration:

Lord, receive my morning worship. I lift my eyes to You as the dawn awakens.

Day 115 – Worship Through the Night

Scripture: *"At midnight I rise to give You thanks because of Your righteous laws."* — Psalm 119:62

Revelation:

Night worship carries intimacy. In the stillness of darkness, hearts commune deeply with God.

Declaration:

Even at midnight, Lord, my praise will rise. My worship watches through the night with You.

Day 116 – Worship in Humility

Scripture: *"God opposes the proud but gives grace to the humble."* — James 4:6

Revelation:

Worship flows through humility. The bowed heart becomes a vessel that grace can fill.

Declaration:

Lord, I humble myself before You. My worship exalts You alone, not me.

Day 117 – Worship of the Redeemer

Scripture: *"Let the redeemed of the Lord say so."* — Psalm 107:2

Revelation:

Redeemed hearts can't stay silent. Worship is the redeemed declaring their rescue with joy.

Declaration:

I am redeemed! I worship You, my Redeemer and Deliverer, forever grateful for Your mercy.

Day 118 – Worship That Ushers Glory

Scripture: *"The earth will be filled with the knowledge of the glory of the Lord as the waters cover the sea."* — Habakkuk 2:14

Revelation:

Our worship joins heaven's mission—spreading His glory until every heart knows His name.

Declaration:

Let Your glory fill the earth, Lord. Use my worship to carry Your presence everywhere.

Day 119 – Worship that Delights the Heart of God

Scripture: *"The Lord takes delight in His people; He crowns the humble with victory."* — Psalm 149:4

Revelation:

God finds pleasure in the worship of His people. Our adoration becomes His joy.

Declaration:

I worship You, Lord, knowing You delight in me. My praise brings joy to Your heart.

Day 120 – Worship that Never Ends

Scripture: *"Blessing and honour and glory and power be unto Him that sits upon the throne, and unto the Lamb forever and ever."* — Revelation 5:13

Revelation:

Worship is eternal. It began before creation and will continue unending in heaven's courts.

Declaration:

Forever and ever, Lord, I will worship You. My voice joins the eternal song of the Lamb.

Month 5
Days 121–150

Day 121 – Worship in Spirit

Scripture: *"God is Spirit, and those who worship Him must worship in spirit and truth."* — John 4:24

Revelation:

Worship transcends the natural realm. It is the meeting of spirit to Spirit — our hearts touching the very essence of God. True worship cannot be mechanical; it is born from the inner life quickened by His presence.

Declaration:

Today, I worship in Spirit and in truth. My praise rises from a heart alive to God's presence.

Day 122 – The Fragrance of Worship

Scripture: *"For we are to God the fragrance of Christ among those who are being saved."* — 2 Corinthians 2:15

Revelation:

Every act of worship releases a spiritual aroma before the Lord. When our hearts are pure and devoted, heaven inhales the scent of our adoration, just as incense filled the temple of old.

Declaration:

Let my worship be a pleasing fragrance before You, Lord. May my life diffuse the aroma of Christ wherever I go.

Day 123 – Worship in Reverence

Scripture: *"Let us offer to God acceptable worship, with reverence and awe."* — Hebrews 12:28

Revelation:

Reverence anchors worship in humility. When we approach the throne of the Holy One, awe grips our soul — not fear, but wonder at His majesty.
Declaration:
Father, I worship You with reverence and awe. You are holy, and I bow before Your glory.

Day 124 – Songs of Deliverance

Scripture: *"You are my hiding place; You shall preserve me from trouble; You shall surround me with songs of deliverance."* — Psalm 32:7
Revelation:
Worship releases deliverance. When we lift our voices in trust, the Lord surrounds us with melodies that break chains and silence fear.
Declaration:
My worship is my weapon. I am surrounded by songs of deliverance from the Lord.

Day 125 – The Throne Room Sound

Scripture: *"And they sang a new song before the throne…"* — Revelation 14:3
Revelation:
Every throne room sound is unique. Worship in heaven is continual, ever-new, and overflowing with revelation. As we worship, we join that eternal sound.
Declaration:
Today, I lift my voice to join the heavenly song. I declare a new sound before the throne!

Day 126 – The Beauty of Holiness

Scripture: *"Worship the Lord in the beauty of holiness."* — Psalm 29:2
Revelation:
Holiness is not dull — it is radiant beauty revealed

through purity and devotion. Worship unveils the splendor of God's holiness and transforms us into His likeness.

Declaration:

Lord, I behold the beauty of Your holiness and reflect it through my worship.

Day 127 – Worship That Costs

Scripture: *"I will not offer burnt offerings to the Lord my God with that which costs me nothing."* — 2 Samuel 24:24

Revelation:

True worship requires sacrifice — not just of things, but of self. Worship becomes precious when it costs us our pride, comfort, or control.

Declaration:

Lord, I give You costly worship. My heart, my time, my all — they belong to You.

Day 128 – Worship Through Tears

Scripture: *"Those who sow in tears shall reap in joy."* — Psalm 126:5

Revelation:

Even in pain, worship is powerful. Tears can be an offering; grief can become a melody. When we worship through brokenness, heaven receives a song of trust.

Declaration:

Lord, I worship You in my tears. I trust that joy will rise from my sorrow.

Day 129 – The Secret Place of Worship

Scripture: *"He who dwells in the secret place of the Most High shall abide under the shadow of the Almighty."* — Psalm 91:1

Revelation:
The most intimate worship happens in hidden places. In solitude, our hearts are tuned to the whispers of His Spirit.
Declaration:
I find my strength in the secret place. In worship, I dwell beneath Your shadow.

Day 130 – The Humility of Worship

Scripture: *"He must increase, but I must decrease."* — John 3:30
Revelation:
Worship exalts God by lowering self. Every genuine act of praise dethrones ego and places Christ at the center.
Declaration:
Today, I choose humility. May my worship magnify You and not me.

Day 131 – Worship in Obedience

Scripture: *"To obey is better than sacrifice."* — 1 Samuel 15:22
Revelation:
Worship without obedience is noise. God delights in hearts that not only sing His praise but live His Word.
Declaration:
My worship is obedience in action. I will do what pleases You, Lord.

Day 132 – Instruments of Praise

Scripture: *"Praise Him with the harp and lyre."* — Psalm 150:3
Revelation:
Every instrument can glorify God when offered in worship. Whether strings or voice, each sound

becomes a testimony of His worth.
Declaration:
I am an instrument in Your hands, Lord. Play through me a melody that honors You.

Day 133 – Worship that Unites

Scripture: *"With one mind and one voice you may glorify the God and Father of our Lord Jesus Christ."* — Romans 15:6
Revelation:
Worship unites hearts across every difference. When voices blend in one accord, heaven hears a symphony of unity.
Declaration:
Lord, make me one in spirit with others who worship You in truth.

Day 134 – Worship Beyond Words

Scripture: *"Be still, and know that I am God."* — Psalm 46:10
Revelation:
Sometimes silence is the loudest form of worship. When we rest in His presence, our stillness speaks louder than a song.
Declaration:
I quiet my soul before You, Lord. My stillness is worship.

Day 135 – The Strength of Worship

Scripture: *"The joy of the Lord is your strength."* — Nehemiah 8:10
Revelation:
Worship births joy, and joy produces strength. When we delight in God, our inner being is renewed with divine energy.

Declaration:
Today I draw strength from worship. The joy of the Lord empowers me!

Day 136 – Worship and the Word

Scripture: *"Let the word of Christ dwell in you richly... singing psalms, hymns, and spiritual songs."* — Colossians 3:16

Revelation:
Worship and the Word are inseparable. Scripture feeds the song of the Spirit, and worship gives life to the Word within us.

Declaration:
Your Word fills my worship, Lord. I sing from revelation, not routine.

Day 137 – The River of Worship

Scripture: *"And wherever the river goes, every living thing will live."* — Ezekiel 47:9

Revelation:
Worship is like a river that brings life wherever it flows. As we yield to the Spirit's current, dead places come alive.

Declaration:
Lord, let Your river of worship flow through me and bring life around me.

Day 138 – Worship in the Fire

Scripture: *"Our God whom we serve is able to deliver us... but if not, we will not bow to your gods."* — Daniel 3:17–18

Revelation:
Real worship stands firm even in fire. When our devotion is tested, our worship proves genuine.

Declaration:

Even in the fire, I will not bow to another. My worship belongs only to You.

Day 139 – Worship in Expectation

Scripture: *"My soul, wait silently for God alone, for my expectation is from Him."* — Psalm 62:5

Revelation:

Worship positions us for divine encounters. Expectation opens the door to revelation and intimacy.

Declaration:

I worship You, Lord, with expectancy. I believe You will meet me in this moment.

Day 140 – The Eternal Song

Scripture: *"They sang the song of Moses... and the song of the Lamb."* — Revelation 15:3

Revelation:

The worship of heaven spans eternity — from Moses' deliverance to the Lamb's victory. We join an unending anthem of redemption.

Declaration:

I lift my voice in the eternal song of the redeemed. Worthy is the Lamb forever!

Day 141 – Worship that Transforms

Scripture: *"We all, beholding the glory of the Lord, are being transformed into the same image."* — 2 Corinthians 3:18

Revelation:

Every moment of true worship changes us. Gazing at His glory reshapes our character into His likeness.

Declaration:

As I worship, I am transformed. I reflect Your image, Lord.

Day 142 – Worship as Warfare

Scripture: *"Let the high praises of God be in their mouth… to execute vengeance on the enemy."* — Psalm 149:6–7

Revelation:

Worship is not passive — it's a weapon. High praises dismantle strongholds and release divine victory.

Declaration:

My praise is my warfare. I worship and watch my enemies scatter.

Day 143 – The Joyful Sound

Scripture: *"Blessed are the people who know the joyful sound!"* — Psalm 89:15

Revelation:

The sound of worship brings blessing. When we tune into heaven's joy, we walk in divine favor.

Declaration:

I rejoice in the joyful sound! My worship attracts Your blessing, Lord.

Day 144 – Worship that Overflows

Scripture: *"My cup runs over."* — Psalm 23:5

Revelation:

Worship fills us until overflow. When we drink deeply of His presence, His goodness spills into every area of life.

Declaration:

Lord, fill me till my worship overflows with Your presence.

Day 145 – The Wonder of His Name

Scripture: *"Let them praise the name of the Lord, for His name alone is exalted."* — Psalm 148:13

Revelation:
Worship magnifies the Name above all names. His Name carries power, healing, and holiness.
Declaration:
I exalt Your Name, O Lord! All glory and honor belong to You.

Day 146 – Worship in Gratitude

Scripture: *"Enter His gates with thanksgiving."* — Psalm 100:4
Revelation:
Gratitude unlocks the gates of worship. A thankful heart prepares the way for the presence of God.
Declaration:
Today, I worship with thanksgiving. My gratitude opens heaven's gates.

Day 147 – The Offering of Praise

Scripture: *"Let us continually offer the sacrifice of praise to God."* — Hebrews 13:15
Revelation:
Worship is not seasonal — it's continual. Every moment is an altar where praise can rise.
Declaration:
I offer You continual praise, Lord — my heart is Your altar.

Day 148 – Worship that Invites Glory

Scripture: *"The glory of the Lord filled the house."* — 2 Chronicles 5:14
Revelation:
When true worship ascends, glory descends. God inhabits the praises of His people, and His presence fills every surrendered space.

Declaration:
Lord, fill this place with Your glory as I worship You.

Day 149 – Worship through Waiting

Scripture: *"Those who wait on the Lord shall renew their strength."* — Isaiah 40:31
Revelation:
Waiting is worship when it's filled with trust. Delays are not denials; they are altars of dependence.
Declaration:
I worship You in my waiting. My strength is renewed as I trust You.

Day 150 – Crowned with Praise

Scripture: *"He crowns the humble with salvation."* — Psalm 149:4
Revelation:
Every worshipper who bows in humility is crowned with grace. Heaven honors those who exalt Him above all.
Declaration:
I lay my crown before You, Lord, and receive the crown of Your salvation.

Month 6
Days 151–180

Day 151 – Worship from the Heart

Scripture: *"This people honors Me with their lips, but their heart is far from Me."* — Matthew 15:8

Revelation:
God is not moved by words alone — He looks for hearts that beat with love for Him. True worship is sincere affection, not mere recitation.

Declaration:
Lord, I worship You from my heart, not from habit. My devotion is real, my love is true.

Day 152 – The Language of Worship

Scripture: *"They spoke in other tongues as the Spirit gave them utterance."* — Acts 2:4

Revelation:
Heaven has a language of worship that flows from the Spirit, not intellect. When we yield, our spirit communicates mysteries to God.

Declaration:
Holy Spirit, fill my mouth with heaven's language. Let my worship transcend words and touch eternity.

Day 153 – Worship that Draws Near

Scripture: *"Draw near to God and He will draw near to you."* — James 4:8

Revelation:
Worship is a movement — as we draw near, God responds with His presence. The distance disappears where adoration begins.

Declaration:

I draw near to You in worship, Lord. I welcome Your nearness and rest in Your embrace.

Day 154 – The Posture of Bowing

Scripture: *"Come, let us bow down in worship, let us kneel before the Lord our Maker."* — Psalm 95:6

Revelation:

Bowing is an act of surrender. When the knees bend, the heart follows — acknowledging His Lordship and majesty.

Declaration:

I bow before You, my Maker. My heart and my body declare — You alone are worthy.

Day 155 – Worship That Opens Heaven

Scripture: *"When Solomon finished praying, fire came down from heaven… and the glory of the Lord filled the temple."* — 2 Chronicles 7:1

Revelation:

When worship rises in purity, heaven responds with glory. God manifests where He is truly adored.

Declaration:

Lord, let my worship open the heavens. Let Your glory fill my life as it filled the temple.

Day 156 – Worship as Surrender

Scripture: *"Present your bodies a living sacrifice, holy, acceptable to God."* — Romans 12:1

Revelation:

Worship is a lifestyle of surrender. Our bodies, choices, and actions become daily offerings of love.

Declaration:

I yield myself as a living sacrifice. My worship is my surrender, my obedience my song.

Day 157 – Worship in Spirit Unity

Scripture: *"Endeavoring to keep the unity of the Spirit in the bond of peace."* — Ephesians 4:3

Revelation:

Worship binds believers in oneness. The same Spirit that fills one fills all, harmonizing hearts in divine unity.

Declaration:

Holy Spirit, make me an instrument of unity. I worship in oneness with Your people.

Day 158 – Worship That Waits

Scripture: *"Truly my soul silently waits for God; from Him comes my salvation."* — Psalm 62:1

Revelation:

Worship isn't hurried. Waiting in His presence is part of adoration — where stillness becomes sacred.

Declaration:

I will wait in worship, Lord. My silence speaks louder than words — You are my desire.

Day 159 – Worship That Lifts Burdens

Scripture: *"The anointing breaks the yoke."* — Isaiah 10:27

Revelation:

Worship releases the anointing that breaks chains. As we exalt Him, heaviness lifts and freedom flows.

Declaration:

I worship until every burden breaks. The anointing of Your presence sets me free.

Day 160 – The Radiance of Worship

Scripture: *"Those who look to Him are radiant."* — Psalm 34:5

Revelation:

Worship changes our countenance. Those who gaze on the Lord reflect His light and carry His glory.

Declaration:

As I worship, Your light shines through me. I radiate Your glory to the world.

Day 161 – Worship That Builds Altars

Scripture: *"Then Noah built an altar to the Lord."* — Genesis 8:20

Revelation:

Altars are places of encounter. Every time we worship, we build a spiritual altar where heaven and earth meet.

Declaration:

Lord, I build an altar of worship in my heart. Let Your fire fall upon it continually.

Day 162 – Worship That Hears

Scripture: *"Speak, Lord, for Your servant is listening."* — 1 Samuel 3:10

Revelation:

Worship is not only expression but also listening. In stillness, God's voice often follows our praise.

Declaration:

I worship and I listen. Your presence is my classroom, and Your word my delight.

Day 163 – Worship That Heals

Scripture: *"As they ministered to the Lord and fasted…"* — Acts 13:2

Revelation:

Ministering to God in worship often ministers healing to us. His presence restores broken hearts and renews weary souls.

Declaration:
As I minister to You, Lord, Your presence heals me from within.

Day 164 – Worship in Weakness

Scripture: *"My strength is made perfect in weakness."* — 2 Corinthians 12:9
Revelation:
Worship isn't hindered by weakness — it's magnified through it. When we feel empty, His grace fills the space.
Declaration:
I bring You my weakness, Lord, and worship You in dependence. Your strength is my song.

Day 165 – Worship That Anchors

Scripture: *"We have this hope as an anchor for the soul."* — Hebrews 6:19
Revelation:
In storms, worship steadies the heart. Praise anchors us in faith when everything around seems uncertain.
Declaration:
Worship anchors my soul. I hold firm to Your presence, Lord, through every storm.

Day 166 – Worship Through Giving

Scripture: *"They opened their treasures and presented gifts to Him."* — Matthew 2:11
Revelation:
The wise still worship through giving. Every offering becomes a declaration of love and honor to the King.
Declaration:
I bring You my treasures, Lord — my time, talent, and heart. All belong to You.

Day 167 – Worship That Exalts the Word

Scripture: *"For You have magnified Your word above all Your name."* — Psalm 138:2

Revelation:

Worship aligns with God's Word. His promises fuel our praise, and our faith-filled worship honors His truth.

Declaration:

Your Word gives life to my worship. I exalt Your truth with my praise.

Day 168 – Worship Through Battle

Scripture: *"Jehoshaphat appointed singers… and when they began to sing and praise, the Lord set ambushes."* — 2 Chronicles 20:21–22

Revelation:

Worship shifts the battlefield. Praise confuses the enemy and invites divine intervention.

Declaration:

I worship in the middle of battle. My song summons victory from heaven.

Day 169 – Worship That Remembers

Scripture: *"Forget not all His benefits."* — Psalm 103:2

Revelation:

Remembrance fuels worship. When we recall God's faithfulness, gratitude ignites afresh.

Declaration:

I remember Your goodness, Lord, and worship with a grateful heart.

Day 170 – Worship That Rises Early

Scripture: *"Early will I seek You."* — Psalm 63:1

Revelation:

The first moments of the day belong to Him. Morning worship sets the rhythm of heaven for the hours ahead.

Declaration:

I rise early to worship You, Lord. My first breath and thought belong to You.

Day 171 – Worship That Overcomes Fear

Scripture: *"I sought the Lord, and He heard me, and delivered me from all my fears."* — Psalm 34:4

Revelation:

Worship expels fear. When we focus on His greatness, our fears shrink and peace fills the soul.

Declaration:

As I worship, fear fades. I am safe in Your presence, Lord.

Day 172 – Worship That Restores Joy

Scripture: *"Restore to me the joy of Your salvation."* — Psalm 51:12

Revelation:

Worship revives joy that sin or sorrow drains away. It resets our heart to divine delight.

Declaration:

Lord, restore my joy through worship. Let my song dance again before You.

Day 173 – Worship That Invites the King

Scripture: *"Lift up your heads, O you gates… and the King of glory shall come in."* — Psalm 24:7

Revelation:

Worship is the key that welcomes the King. Every lifted heart becomes a gate through which glory enters.

Declaration:

I open my heart wide. Come in, King of glory — You are welcome here.

Day 174 – Worship That Redeems Time

Scripture: *"Redeeming the time, because the days are evil."* — Ephesians 5:16

Revelation:

Time spent in worship is never wasted — it is invested. God restores and multiplies moments we surrender to Him.

Declaration:

I redeem my time through worship. Every second spent with You bears eternal fruit.

Day 175 – Worship That Celebrates His Faithfulness

Scripture: *"Your faithfulness reaches to the clouds."* — Psalm 36:5

Revelation:

Worship celebrates consistency — the steadfast love that never fails. Our praise mirrors His unwavering nature.

Declaration:

Lord, You are faithful through every season. I worship You for Your unchanging love.

Day 176 – Worship That Births Vision

Scripture: *"I saw the Lord, high and exalted."* — Isaiah 6:1

Revelation:

True vision comes in worship. When eyes are lifted to behold Him, we see life from heaven's perspective.

Declaration:

As I worship, I see You clearly, Lord. Open my eyes to behold Your glory.

Day 177 – Worship That Cultivates Peace

Scripture: *"You will keep him in perfect peace, whose mind is stayed on You."* — Isaiah 26:3

Revelation:

Worship stills the mind and anchors peace. The more we fix our thoughts on Him, the quieter life's noise becomes.

Declaration:

I fix my heart on You, Lord. My worship ushers in Your perfect peace.

Day 178 – Worship That Delights the Father

Scripture: *"The Father seeks those who will worship Him in spirit and truth."* — John 4:23

Revelation:

Of all that God could desire, He seeks worshippers. Our worship brings joy to His heart and fulfills His longing for fellowship.

Declaration:

Father, I am Yours. May my worship delight Your heart today.

Day 179 – Worship That Endures

Scripture: *"I will bless the Lord at all times; His praise shall continually be in my mouth."* — Psalm 34:1

Revelation:

Enduring worship is constant, not circumstantial. It remains steady through both triumph and trial.

Declaration:

I will bless You at all times, Lord. My praise will never cease.

Day 180 – Worship That Invites Glory's Weight

Scripture: *"The priests could not stand to minister because of the cloud."* — 1 Kings 8:11

Revelation:

There is a worship so deep that it ushers the tangible weight of God's presence — His glory overwhelms human strength.

Declaration:

Let Your glory fill this temple, Lord. I surrender beneath the weight of Your presence.

Month 7
Days 181–210

Day 181 – Worship That Seeks His Face

Scripture: *"When You said, 'Seek My face,' my heart said to You, 'Your face, Lord, I will seek.'"* — Psalm 27:8

Revelation:
Worship is not content with blessings; it seeks the Blesser. The true worshipper desires the face of God more than His hand.

Declaration:
Lord, I seek not Your gifts but Your face. My worship is the pursuit of Your presence.

Day 182 – Worship That Exalts His Throne

Scripture: *"The Lord is enthroned on the praises of Israel."* — Psalm 22:3

Revelation:
Praise creates a throne for God's presence. Wherever worship rises, His rule is established.

Declaration:
Be enthroned upon my praise today, Lord. Reign over my life as I exalt You.

Day 183 – Worship in the Midst of Chaos

Scripture: *"When the earth totters, and all its inhabitants, it is I who keep steady its pillars."* — Psalm 75:3

Revelation:
In chaos, worship restores order. Declaring His sovereignty anchors our hearts in stability.

Declaration:

Even when the world shakes, I worship You. You hold all things together, Lord.

Day 184 – Worship That Produces Intimacy

Scripture: *"The secret of the Lord is with those who fear Him."* — Psalm 25:14

Revelation:

Worship draws us into divine secrets. Intimacy is birthed in reverence; those who truly adore Him are invited closer.

Declaration:

Lord, draw me near to Your heart. I long to know You through worship's intimacy.

Day 185 – Worship That Stills the Enemy

Scripture: *"From the mouths of infants You have ordained praise to silence the foe and the avenger."* — Psalm 8:2

Revelation:

Even the simplest worship silences darkness. Praise paralyzes the enemy's plans and releases divine defense.

Declaration:

My worship silences every voice of accusation. The sound of praise defeats my adversary.

Day 186 – Worship That Burns with Passion

Scripture: *"Did not our hearts burn within us while He talked with us on the road?"* — Luke 24:32

Revelation:

True worship ignites holy passion. As His presence draws near, our hearts blaze with living fire.

Declaration:

Set my heart ablaze with worship, Lord. Let my passion for You never fade.

Day 187 – Worship That Humbles the Soul

Scripture: *"Humble yourselves in the sight of the Lord, and He will lift you up."* — James 4:10
Revelation:
The higher we go in worship, the lower we bow in humility. God elevates those who lay low before His glory.
Declaration:
I humble myself before You, Lord. Exalt Yourself through my worship.

Day 188 – Worship That Abides

Scripture: *"Abide in Me, and I in you."* — John 15:4
Revelation:
Worship is not an event; it's an abiding relationship. Those who dwell in Him carry a continual awareness of His presence.
Declaration:
I abide in You, Lord. My life is one long song of worship in Your presence.

Day 189 – Worship in the Wilderness

Scripture: *"He led you through the great and terrible wilderness… that He might humble and test you."* — Deuteronomy 8:15–16
Revelation:
Wilderness worship refines the heart. When comfort fades, true devotion is revealed.
Declaration:
Even in the wilderness, I will worship You. My song will not cease in barren places.

Day 190 – Worship That Overflows with Gratitude

Scripture: *"In everything give thanks; for this is the will of God."* — 1 Thessalonians 5:18

Revelation:
Gratitude transforms ordinary moments into worship. Thanksgiving tunes our hearts to heaven's frequency.

Declaration:
Lord, thank You for all You are and all You've done. My worship overflows with gratitude.

Day 191 – Worship That Stands in Awe

Scripture: *"Stand still and consider the wondrous works of God."* — Job 37:14

Revelation:
Awe is the heart of worship. When we behold His wonders, silence becomes sacred.

Declaration:
I stand in awe of You, Lord. My worship springs from wonder.

Day 192 – Worship That Brings Revelation

Scripture: *"I was in the Spirit on the Lord's Day, and I heard behind me a loud voice like a trumpet."* — Revelation 1:10

Revelation:
Revelation flows from worship. When we're lost in adoration, heaven often opens to reveal divine mysteries.

Declaration:
Lord, open my eyes as I worship. Reveal Your heart to me through Your Spirit.

Day 193 – Worship That Marks a Generation

Scripture: *"One generation shall praise Your works to another."* — Psalm 145:4

Revelation:

Worship leaves a legacy. Our adoration inspires the next generation to know and honor God.

Declaration:

May my worship mark generations to come, Lord. Let my song echo beyond my years.

Day 194 – Worship That Transcends Culture

Scripture: *"All nations whom You have made shall come and worship before You."* — Psalm 86:9

Revelation:

True worship unites nations under one King. In His presence, every language becomes one sound.

Declaration:

Lord, I join the nations in worship. Every tongue shall declare Your glory!

Day 195 – Worship That Births Revival

Scripture: *"When they lifted up their voice… the house was filled with the glory of the Lord."* — 2 Chronicles 5:13

Revelation:

Revival begins with worship. When hearts unite in pure adoration, heaven's glory invades earth.

Declaration:

Let revival start in my worship, Lord. Fill this place with Your glory!

Day 196 – Worship That Lifts the Broken

Scripture: *"A bruised reed He will not break."* — Isaiah 42:3

Revelation:

God cherishes the worship of the broken. When we come as we are, His love restores and strengthens us.

Declaration:

Lord, I bring You my brokenness. Receive my imperfect worship and make me whole.

Day 197 – Worship That Awakens Hope

Scripture: *"Why are you cast down, O my soul?… Hope in God, for I shall yet praise Him."* — Psalm 42:11

Revelation:

Worship revives hope in despair. Praising through pain shifts our focus from the valley to the Victor.

Declaration:

I will yet praise You, Lord! My worship awakens hope within me.

Day 198 – Worship That Exalts His Word

Scripture: *"The entrance of Your words gives light."* — Psalm 119:130

Revelation:

Worship and Word walk hand in hand. The more we adore Him, the clearer His Word becomes.

Declaration:

Illuminate me through Your Word, Lord. I worship You, the Living Word.

Day 199 – Worship That Touches Eternity

Scripture: *"Holy, holy, holy, is the Lord God Almighty, who was and is and is to come."* —

Revelation 4:8
Revelation:
Worship is eternal language. Every time we worship, we echo heaven's ceaseless anthem.
Declaration:
I join eternity's song — holy, holy, holy is the Lord!

Day 200 – Worship That Reflects His Image

Scripture: *"As we behold… we are being transformed into the same image from glory to glory."* — 2 Corinthians 3:18
Revelation:
Worship changes what we behold into what we become. Gazing at His beauty shapes us into His likeness.
Declaration:
As I worship, I am transformed. May Your image be seen in me.

Day 201 – Worship That Invites the Cloud

Scripture: *"The cloud covered the tent of meeting, and the glory of the Lord filled the tabernacle."* — Exodus 40:34
Revelation:
Where worship is pure, glory rests. The cloud of His presence is drawn to sincere adoration.
Declaration:
Lord, fill this temple with Your cloud. Let Your glory dwell in my worship.

Day 202 – Worship That Declares His Sovereignty

Scripture: *"The Lord reigns; let the earth rejoice!"* — Psalm 97:1

Revelation:
Worship is a royal proclamation. Every declaration of His reign invites His authority to manifest on earth.
Declaration:
You reign, O Lord! My worship declares Your sovereign rule.

Day 203 – Worship That Stirs Heaven's Joy

Scripture: *"There is joy before the angels of God over one sinner who repents."* — Luke 15:10
Revelation:
Heaven rejoices not just at salvation but at every moment of genuine worship. Our songs become part of heaven's celebration.
Declaration:
Let my worship bring joy to heaven, Lord. May angels dance to the melody of my praise.

Day 204 – Worship That Births Rest

Scripture: *"My presence will go with you, and I will give you rest."* — Exodus 33:14
Revelation:
Worship ushers us into divine rest. In His presence, striving ceases and peace reigns.
Declaration:
I rest in Your presence, Lord. My worship is my resting place.

Day 205 – Worship That Lifts the Soul

Scripture: *"Bless the Lord, O my soul, and all that is within me."* — Psalm 103:1
Revelation:
When the soul feels heavy, worship lifts it upward. Speaking to our own hearts stirs forgotten praise.

Declaration:
Soul, rise and worship the Lord! Every part of me blesses His name.

Day 206 – Worship That Strengthens Faith

Scripture: *"Abraham did not waver in unbelief but grew strong in faith, giving glory to God."* — Romans 4:20
Revelation:
Faith grows in worship. Glorifying God in the waiting strengthens trust in His promises.
Declaration:
I give You glory in faith, Lord. My worship strengthens my belief in You.

Day 207 – Worship That Celebrates the Cross

Scripture: *"Worthy is the Lamb who was slain!"* — Revelation 5:12
Revelation:
The cross is the center of all worship. Every song and sacrifice finds its meaning in the Lamb's victory.
Declaration:
Worthy is the Lamb! My worship celebrates Your finished work, Jesus.

Day 208 – Worship That Opens the Eyes

Scripture: *"Then their eyes were opened, and they knew Him."* — Luke 24:31
Revelation:
In worship, blindness fades. When we behold Him rightly, revelation dawns and truth unfolds.
Declaration:
Open my eyes, Lord, as I worship. Let me see You as You are.

Day 209 – Worship That Echoes Heaven

Scripture: *"On earth as it is in heaven."* — Matthew 6:10

Revelation:

Worship is heaven's culture expressed on earth. Every act of adoration aligns us with eternity's rhythm.

Declaration:

Lord, let my worship echo heaven's sound. As it is in heaven, so be it here.

Day 210 – Worship That Pleases the King

Scripture: *"The Lord takes pleasure in His people; He will beautify the humble with salvation."* — Psalm 149:4

Revelation:

God delights in worship that comes from humility. He crowns the meek with beauty and salvation.

Declaration:

Lord, may my humble worship please You. I offer You the beauty of my surrendered heart.

Month 8
Days 211–240

Day 211 – Worship That Thrills Heaven

Scripture: *"Let everything that has breath praise the Lord!"* — Psalm 150:6

Revelation:
Every breath is a gift designed for praise. Heaven thrills when the earth resounds with life-filled worship.

Declaration:
Lord, my breath belongs to You. Let every inhale and exhale declare Your praise.

Day 212 – Worship That Recognizes His Majesty

Scripture: *"Splendor and majesty are before Him; strength and beauty are in His sanctuary."* — Psalm 96:6

Revelation:
Worship unveils God's majesty. When we behold His grandeur, our hearts bow in holy wonder.

Declaration:
Majestic King, I worship You in beauty and strength. You are clothed in glory forever!

Day 213 – Worship That Shakes the Foundations

Scripture: *"Suddenly there was a great earthquake… and everyone's chains were loosed."* — Acts 16:26

Revelation:
Worship breaks strongholds and shakes spiritual prisons. Praise becomes a key that unlocks freedom.

Declaration:

My worship breaks chains today! Every wall trembles before Your mighty presence, Lord.

Day 214 – Worship That Delights His Heart

Scripture: *"The Lord takes delight in His people."* — Psalm 149:4
Revelation:
Worship is more than sound — it's affection. The Father delights when our hearts sing from pure love.
Declaration:
I worship You, Lord, not for what You give but for who You are. Let my love bring You delight.

Day 215 – Worship That Echoes Through Generations

Scripture: *"From the rising of the sun to its setting, the name of the Lord is to be praised."* — Psalm 113:3
Revelation:
Worship is an unending cycle — as one voice fades, another rises. From dawn to dusk, praise never stops.
Declaration:
May my worship echo from this generation to the next. Let Your name be praised forever, Lord!

Day 216 – Worship That Offers the Best

Scripture: *"Honor the Lord with your wealth, with the firstfruits of all your crops."* — Proverbs 3:9
Revelation:
True worship gives its best. Whether time, talent, or treasure, God deserves our first and finest.
Declaration:
Lord, I give You my best — not leftovers but firstfruits. My worship honors You above all.

Day 217 – Worship That Flows from Love

Scripture: *"We love Him because He first loved us."* — 1 John 4:19

Revelation:

Worship is love responding to love. It begins not with duty but with the overflow of a grateful heart.

Declaration:

Your love compels my worship, Lord. I adore You because You first loved me.

Day 218 – Worship That Waits on God

Scripture: *"Be still before the Lord and wait patiently for Him."* — Psalm 37:7

Revelation:

Waiting is worship too. Silence in His presence speaks louder than hurried words.

Declaration:

I will wait for You, Lord. My stillness is my worship — I trust in Your timing.

Day 219 – Worship That Overcomes Fear

Scripture: *"I sought the Lord, and He answered me; He delivered me from all my fears."* — Psalm 34:4

Revelation:

Fear flees where worship reigns. Adoration shifts focus from problems to the Almighty.

Declaration:

As I worship, fear melts away. My heart is steadfast, trusting in You, Lord.

Day 220 – Worship That Touches the Nations

Scripture: *"All the ends of the earth will remember and turn to the Lord."* — Psalm 22:27

Revelation:
Worship carries global power. Every sincere song has the potential to awaken hearts across borders.
Declaration:
Let my worship reach the nations, Lord. Let every tribe and tongue glorify Your name.

Day 221 – Worship That Flows from Obedience

Scripture: *"To obey is better than sacrifice."* — 1 Samuel 15:22
Revelation:
Obedience is the melody heaven loves most. Worship without surrender is noise, but obedience sings truth.
Declaration:
Lord, let my obedience be my worship. I yield to Your will in joyful surrender.

Day 222 – Worship That Guards the Heart

Scripture: *"Keep your heart with all diligence, for out of it spring the issues of life."* — Proverbs 4:23
Revelation:
Worship keeps the heart pure. When we gaze on His holiness, our inner life is cleansed and guarded.
Declaration:
Purify my heart in worship, Lord. Keep me centered in Your presence always.

Day 223 – Worship That Celebrates His Faithfulness

Scripture: *"Your faithfulness endures to all generations."* — Psalm 119:90
Revelation:
Worship recalls His faithfulness. Remembering what

He's done fans the flames of adoration.

Declaration:
You have never failed me, Lord. I worship You for Your enduring faithfulness.

Day 224 – Worship That Releases Joy

Scripture: *"In Your presence is fullness of joy."* — Psalm 16:11

Revelation:
Joy is heaven's atmosphere, and worship is its doorway. In His presence, sorrow loses its voice.

Declaration:
My joy flows from Your presence, Lord. I rejoice in worship today!

Day 225 – Worship That Proclaims His Greatness

Scripture: *"Great is the Lord and greatly to be praised."* — Psalm 145:3

Revelation:
Worship declares what words cannot measure — His greatness beyond comprehension.

Declaration:
You are greater than my thoughts, Lord. My worship proclaims Your unmatched greatness.

Day 226 – Worship That Is Holy

Scripture: *"Worship the Lord in the beauty of holiness."* — Psalm 29:2

Revelation:
Holiness beautifies worship. When the heart is set apart for Him, our offering carries divine fragrance.

Declaration:
Lord, I worship You in the beauty of holiness. Let my life be pure incense before You.

Day 227 – Worship That Invites Transformation

Scripture: *"Be transformed by the renewing of your mind."* — Romans 12:2

Revelation:

True worship transforms the mind. As we behold Him, our thoughts align with heaven's patterns.

Declaration:

Renew me, Lord, as I worship. Change my mind to reflect Your glory.

Day 228 – Worship That Draws the Hungry

Scripture: *"O taste and see that the Lord is good!"* — Psalm 34:8

Revelation:

Worship is contagious. When we adore Him openly, others are drawn to taste His goodness too.

Declaration:

Let my worship make others hunger for You, Lord. May they see Your goodness through my praise.

Day 229 – Worship That Fills the House

Scripture: *"The temple was filled with the cloud."* — 2 Chronicles 5:14

Revelation:

When united hearts worship, glory fills the house. His manifest presence responds to collective adoration.

Declaration:

Fill this place with Your glory, Lord. Let every heart become a temple of praise!

Day 230 – Worship That Springs from Mercy

Scripture: *"I will sing of the mercies of the Lord forever."* — Psalm 89:1

Revelation:

Every note of worship is born from mercy. Knowing we're forgiven gives our praise its sweetest tone.

Declaration:

Because of Your mercy, I sing forever, Lord. My worship rises from Your grace.

Day 231 – Worship That Celebrates His Name

Scripture: *"Blessed be the name of the Lord from this time forth and forevermore!"* — Psalm 113:2

Revelation:

His Name is worthy of endless adoration. Worship exalts the unchanging, ever-holy Name of the Lord.

Declaration:

Blessed be Your Name, O Lord! My lips will forever exalt You.

Day 232 – Worship That Births Unity

Scripture: *"Behold, how good and pleasant it is when brothers dwell in unity."* — Psalm 133:1

Revelation:

True worship unites hearts. Where love and harmony dwell, God commands His blessing.

Declaration:

Unite us, Lord, in worship. Let our one voice bring joy to Your heart.

Day 233 – Worship That Invites Heaven's Fire

Scripture: *"Fire came out from before the Lord and consumed the offering."* — Leviticus 9:24

Revelation:

When worship is pure, God answers with fire. His presence consumes and consecrates.

Declaration:

Send Your holy fire, Lord. Let my worship be an altar that burns for You.

Day 234 – Worship That Prospers the Spirit

Scripture: *"Beloved, I pray that you may prosper in all things and be in health, just as your soul prospers."* — 3 John 1:2

Revelation:

Worship nourishes the soul, and a prospering soul overflows into every area of life.

Declaration:

As I worship, my soul prospers. My spirit flourishes in Your presence, Lord.

Day 235 – Worship That Looks Heavenward

Scripture: *"I lift up my eyes to the hills—where does my help come from?"* — Psalm 121:1

Revelation:

Worship lifts our gaze. When eyes fix on heaven, earthly burdens lose their power.

Declaration:

My eyes are fixed on You, Lord. I worship the Maker of heaven and earth.

Day 236 – Worship That Honors the Creator

Scripture: *"For by Him all things were created… all things were created through Him and for Him."* — Colossians 1:16

Revelation:
Creation exists to worship its Creator. Every living thing was formed to give Him glory.

Declaration:
I was made for You, Lord. My purpose is to worship my Creator forever.

Day 237 – Worship That Waits for His Glory

Scripture: *"My soul waits for the Lord more than watchmen for the morning."* — Psalm 130:6

Revelation:
The waiting heart of a worshipper longs for His glory to break like dawn. Patience becomes praise in the process.

Declaration:
I wait for You, Lord, in worshipful expectation. Let Your glory arise upon me.

Day 238 – Worship That Honors His Holiness

Scripture: *"Exalt the Lord our God and worship at His footstool; He is holy."* — Psalm 99:5

Revelation:
Holiness demands reverence. Worship recognizes His otherness — majestic, pure, unapproachable yet near.

Declaration:

Holy are You, Lord! I bow at Your feet in awe and reverence.

Day 239 – Worship That Is Continual

Scripture: *"I will bless the Lord at all times; His praise shall continually be in my mouth."* — Psalm 34:1

Revelation:

Worship is a lifestyle, not a moment. Continual praise keeps the heart tuned to heaven.

Declaration:

Your praise will never leave my lips, Lord. I will worship You at all times.

Day 240 – Worship That Crown Him Lord of All

Scripture: *"On His robe and on His thigh He has a name written, King of kings and Lord of lords."* — Revelation 19:16

Revelation:

Every act of worship is a coronation. When we exalt Jesus, we crown Him Lord again in our hearts.

Declaration:

You are my King and my Lord forever. Be crowned upon my worship, Jesus!

Month 9
Days 241–270

Day 241 – Worship That Exalts the Unseen God

Scripture: *“No one has ever seen God; but if we love one another, God lives in us.”* — 1 John 4:12

Revelation:
Worship reaches beyond sight. We adore the invisible God who reveals Himself in love.

Declaration:
Though unseen, You are more real than all I know. I worship You, Eternal One.

Day 242 – Worship That Brings Heaven Near

Scripture: *“Your kingdom come, Your will be done on earth as it is in heaven.”* — Matthew 6:10

Revelation:
Worship invites heaven to earth. Each moment of adoration makes the atmosphere of God tangible.

Declaration:
Lord, let my worship draw heaven near. May Your will and glory fill my space.

Day 243 – Worship That Surrenders All

Scripture: *“Present your bodies as a living sacrifice, holy and acceptable to God.”* — Romans 12:1

Revelation:
Worship is surrender — offering not just lips, but life. The altar of worship demands our all.

Declaration:
Here I am, Lord — my life is Yours. I worship You with everything I am.

Day 244 – Worship That Proclaims His Power

Scripture: *"Yours, O Lord, is the greatness and the power and the glory."* — 1 Chronicles 29:11

Revelation:

Worship magnifies God's might. Every proclamation of His power dethrones fear and exalts faith.

Declaration:

You are mighty, Lord! My worship declares Your power and glory in all the earth.

Day 245 – Worship That Waits for His Whisper

Scripture: *"After the fire came a gentle whisper."* — 1 Kings 19:12

Revelation:

In the quiet moments of worship, His whisper is heard. Stillness reveals His voice more clearly than noise.

Declaration:

I wait for Your whisper, Lord. In silence and awe, I worship and listen.

Day 246 – Worship That Purifies the Soul

Scripture: *"Draw near to God and He will draw near to you. Cleanse your hands, you sinners."* — James 4:8

Revelation:

Approaching God in worship cleanses the heart. The nearness of His holiness refines our souls.

Declaration:

As I draw near, purify me, Lord. Let my worship flow from a clean heart.

Day 247 – Worship That Honors His Covenant

Scripture: *"He remembers His covenant forever."* — Psalm 105:8

Revelation:
Every song of worship recalls His unbroken promise. Praise reminds us that His faithfulness never ends.

Declaration:
You are the Covenant-Keeping God! My worship celebrates Your eternal promise.

Day 248 – Worship That Overflows from Gratitude

Scripture: *"Enter His gates with thanksgiving and His courts with praise."* — Psalm 100:4

Revelation:
Gratitude is the gateway to worship. A thankful heart never runs out of songs.

Declaration:
With gratitude, I enter Your presence, Lord. My worship flows from thanksgiving.

Day 249 – Worship That Declares His Beauty

Scripture: *"One thing I ask... to gaze on the beauty of the Lord."* — Psalm 27:4

Revelation:
Worship beholds divine beauty. The more we gaze, the more we are captivated by His splendor.

Declaration:
You are beautiful beyond description, Lord. My heart worships in wonder of You.

Day 250 – Worship That Opens the Heavens

Scripture: *"Heaven opened, and I saw the Spirit descending like a dove."* — Matthew 3:16

Revelation:

Heaven responds to pure worship. When adoration rises, revelation descends.

Declaration:

Lord, open the heavens as I worship. Let Your Spirit rest upon me.

Day 251 – Worship That Beholds His Glory

Scripture: *"Show me Your glory."* — Exodus 33:18

Revelation:

Worship yearns to see His glory — the radiance of His being revealed to the heart that truly seeks.

Declaration:

Show me Your glory, Lord. My worship is the cry of a heart that longs for You.

Day 252 – Worship That Anchors the Heart

Scripture: *"My heart is fixed, O God, my heart is steadfast; I will sing and give praise."* — Psalm 57:7

Revelation:

Worship stabilizes us amid storms. A steadfast heart cannot be shaken when anchored in adoration.

Declaration:

My heart is fixed on You, Lord. My worship anchors me in Your unchanging truth.

Day 253 – Worship That Honors His Voice

Scripture: *"Today, if you hear His voice, do not harden your hearts."* — Psalm 95:7–8

Revelation:

True worship listens. The song that pleases God

most is obedience to His voice.

Declaration:

Speak, Lord — Your servant worships and obeys. My heart is open to Your word.

Day 254 – Worship That Awakens the Dawn

Scripture: *"Awake, my soul! I will awaken the dawn."* — Psalm 57:8

Revelation:

Worship brings light to dark places. The praises of the righteous herald new beginnings.

Declaration:

With my song, I awaken the dawn. Lord, let worship light up my morning.

Day 255 – Worship That Triumphs Over Trials

Scripture: *"Count it all joy when you fall into various trials."* — James 1:2

Revelation:

Worship turns pain into praise. When we glorify Him in hardship, victory begins.

Declaration:

Even in trial, I worship You, Lord. My song declares that You are greater.

Day 256 – Worship That Sees the King

Scripture: *"I saw the Lord sitting on a throne, high and lifted up."* — Isaiah 6:1

Revelation:

In worship, vision clears — we see the King exalted above all. Adoration opens heaven's view.

Declaration:
I behold You, O King of Glory. You are high and lifted up in my worship.

Day 257 – Worship That Touches His Heart

Scripture: *"Mary took a pound of costly ointment and anointed His feet."* — John 12:3
Revelation:
Worship that costs something moves His heart deeply. Extravagant love is never wasted on Jesus.
Declaration:
I pour out my worship, Lord. Nothing is too precious for the One I love.

Day 258 – Worship That Flows in Spirit and Truth

Scripture: *"True worshipers will worship the Father in spirit and truth."* — John 4:23
Revelation:
Worship in spirit connects with heaven; worship in truth aligns with the Word. Together, they please the Father.
Declaration:
I worship You, Lord, in spirit and in truth — with heart and understanding united.

Day 259 – Worship That Calls the Nations

Scripture: *"Let the peoples praise You, O God; let all the peoples praise You!"* — Psalm 67:3
Revelation:
Worship is a global invitation. When we praise, we call the earth to join heaven's song.
Declaration:

Let every nation praise You, Lord! My worship joins the chorus of creation.

Day 260 – Worship That Rebuilds Altars

Scripture: *"Elijah repaired the altar of the Lord that was broken down."* — 1 Kings 18:30

Revelation:

Where altars are restored, fire returns. Worship rebuilds what neglect has broken.

Declaration:

Lord, rebuild the altar of my heart. Let true worship rise again in me.

Day 261 – Worship That Dwells in His Courts

Scripture: *"Blessed are those who dwell in Your house; they are ever praising You."* — Psalm 84:4

Revelation:

To dwell in His courts is the highest privilege. Worshipers live where His presence abides continually.

Declaration:

I choose to dwell in Your courts, Lord. My soul delights in Your presence forever.

Day 262 – Worship That Hears His Song

Scripture: *"He will rejoice over you with singing."* — Zephaniah 3:17

Revelation:

In worship, we not only sing — we listen. God sings over His beloved with joy and affection.

Declaration:

Sing over me, Lord. Let my worship be a duet with heaven's melody.

Day 263 – Worship That Invites His Wind

Scripture: *"Suddenly a sound like a mighty rushing wind filled the house."* — Acts 2:2

Revelation:

When worship rises, the Spirit moves. The wind of God breathes life into surrendered hearts.

Declaration:

Come, Holy Spirit — fill my worship with Your wind and breath of life.

Day 264 – Worship That Births Peace

Scripture: *"The Lord bless you and keep you; the Lord make His face shine on you and give you peace."* — Numbers 6:24–26

Revelation:

The face of God brings peace. Worship that beholds His face dispels every storm within.

Declaration:

Lord, as I worship, let Your peace rule my heart. Shine Your face upon me.

Day 265 – Worship That Exalts His Word Above All

Scripture: *"You have magnified Your word above all Your name."* — Psalm 138:2

Revelation:

Worship honors what God honors — His Word. When we exalt Scripture, we align with His heart.

Declaration:

I worship You, Lord, by loving Your Word. Let Your truth shape my praise.

Day 266 – Worship That Stands in the Fire

Scripture: *"The fourth man looked like the Son of God."* — Daniel 3:25

Revelation:
Worship doesn't escape the fire; it meets God in it. The presence of the Son transforms trials into testimonies.
Declaration:
Even in fire, You are with me, Lord. I worship You in the furnace of faith.

Day 267 – Worship That Reflects His Light

Scripture: *"Arise, shine; for your light has come!"* — Isaiah 60:1
Revelation:
Worshipers carry His light. When we adore Him, His glory reflects through our lives.
Declaration:
Shine through me, Lord. Let my worship radiate Your glory in this world.

Day 268 – Worship That Restores Joy to the Broken

Scripture: *"Restore to me the joy of Your salvation."* — Psalm 51:12
Revelation:
Repentant worship restores lost joy. God delights in contrite hearts that sing again.
Declaration:
Restore my joy, Lord. Let my worship rise from a heart made whole.

Day 269 – Worship That Magnifies His Name

Scripture: *"Oh, magnify the Lord with me, and let us exalt His name together."* — Psalm 34:3
Revelation:
Worship enlarges our view of God. The more we

exalt Him, the smaller our problems become.
Declaration:
I magnify You, Lord! Be exalted high above all the earth.

Day 270 – Worship That Joins the Eternal Song

Scripture: *"They sing a new song before the throne."* — Revelation 14:3
Revelation:
Every act of worship on earth joins the unending song of heaven. It is our rehearsal for eternity.
Declaration:
I join heaven's eternal worship today. Holy, holy, holy is the Lord forever!

Month 10
Days 271–300

Day 271 – Worship That Draws the Cloud of Glory

Scripture: *"The house of the Lord was filled with a cloud, so that the priests could not stand to minister."* — 2 Chronicles 5:13–14

Revelation:
When worship unites in purity and harmony, God's glory fills the atmosphere. Human strength bows when heaven invades.

Declaration:
Lord, fill this temple with Your cloud of glory. Let my worship usher in Your presence beyond measure.

Day 272 – Worship That Silences the Enemy

Scripture: *"From the mouths of children You have ordained praise to silence the foe."* — Psalm 8:2

Revelation:
Praise is spiritual warfare. Worship disarms the enemy's voice and establishes divine authority.

Declaration:
Through my worship, Lord, silence every adversary. Let praise be my weapon of victory.

Day 273 – Worship That Flows from Revelation

Scripture: *"You are the Christ, the Son of the living God."* — Matthew 16:16

Revelation:
True worship flows from knowing *who* He is, not what

He gives. Revelation fuels adoration.
Declaration:
You are the Christ, the Living One! My worship springs from revelation of Your glory.

Day 274 – Worship That Hosts His Presence

Scripture: *"The Lord is enthroned upon the praises of Israel."* — Psalm 22:3
Revelation:
Worship builds a throne for God. Wherever praise arises, His presence chooses to dwell.
Declaration:
Be enthroned on my praise, O Lord. Make my life Your dwelling place.

Day 275 – Worship That Overflows Like Oil

Scripture: *"She poured it on His head as He reclined at the table."* — Matthew 26:7
Revelation:
Worship is costly oil — fragrant, poured, and precious. It fills the room with the aroma of devotion.
Declaration:
I pour my worship like oil on You, Jesus. Let its fragrance honor Your name.

Day 276 – Worship That Opens Prison Doors

Scripture: *"At midnight Paul and Silas were praying and singing hymns… and the prison doors flew open."* — Acts 16:25–26
Revelation:
Worship releases divine power in impossible places.

Praise turns prisons into sanctuaries.
Declaration:
Lord, as I worship, open every locked door. Let my praise bring freedom and breakthrough.

Day 277 – Worship That Anticipates His Glory

Scripture: *"We shall be like Him, for we shall see Him as He is."* — 1 John 3:2
Revelation:
Worship is a rehearsal for the day we behold Him in fullness. Every act of adoration prepares us for eternity.
Declaration:
I worship You, Lord, with hope and longing. One day, I will see You face to face.

Day 278 – Worship That Restores Reverence

Scripture: *"Let all the earth fear the Lord; let all the inhabitants stand in awe of Him."* — Psalm 33:8
Revelation:
Worship revives awe in a casual world. It reminds us that God is holy and worthy of trembling honor.
Declaration:
I stand in holy awe before You, Lord. Let reverence return to my worship.

Day 279 – Worship That Becomes a Fragrant Offering

Scripture: *"Your prayers and gifts have come up as a memorial offering before God."* — Acts 10:4
Revelation:
Worship rises like incense — remembered in

heaven. The fragrance of our devotion never fades before God.

Declaration:

Let my worship ascend as fragrance to Your throne, Lord. May it please Your heart forever.

Day 280 – Worship That Sanctifies the Atmosphere

Scripture: *"The glory of the Lord filled the tabernacle."* — Exodus 40:34

Revelation:

When God's presence fills a place, everything becomes holy ground. Worship purifies the air with His glory.

Declaration:

Lord, fill my surroundings with Your presence. Let my worship sanctify every space I enter.

Day 281 – Worship That Draws Living Water

Scripture: *"Out of his heart will flow rivers of living water."* — John 7:38

Revelation:

The flow of worship is like a river — refreshing, unending, and life-giving. His Spirit fills and overflows.

Declaration:

Let Your living waters flow through my worship, Lord. Refresh every dry place within me.

Day 282 – Worship That Reflects His Holiness

Scripture: *"Be holy, for I am holy."* — 1 Peter 1:16

Revelation:

Holiness and worship are inseparable. True adoration imitates the character of the One we behold.

Declaration:

Make me holy, Lord, as I worship. Let my life reflect Your purity and glory.

Day 283 – Worship That Builds Spiritual Strength

Scripture: *"The joy of the Lord is your strength."* — Nehemiah 8:10

Revelation:

Worship strengthens the weary. Joy born in God's presence renews the spirit and sustains the heart.

Declaration:

Your joy is my strength, Lord. As I worship, I am revived in Your presence.

Day 284 – Worship That Stirs the Spirit

Scripture: *"While I was praying, my spirit was stirred within me."* — Daniel 7:15

Revelation:

Worship awakens the spirit to divine realities. It stirs sensitivity to God's movements and whispers.

Declaration:

Stir my spirit, Lord. Let my worship awaken deep communion with You.

Day 285 – Worship That Mirrors Heaven's Order

Scripture: *"Around the throne, they never cease to say, 'Holy, holy, holy.'"* — Revelation 4:8

Revelation:

Heaven's rhythm is unending worship. Earthly adoration aligns us with heaven's eternal pattern.

Declaration:
Let my worship mirror heaven, Lord. May praise never cease from my lips.

Day 286 – Worship That Carries the Fire

Scripture: *"The fire must be kept burning on the altar continuously; it must not go out."* — Leviticus 6:13
Revelation:
The flame of worship must never die. Daily adoration keeps our hearts burning with holy fire.
Declaration:
Keep my altar burning, Lord. Let the fire of worship never go out in me.

Day 287 – Worship That Reveals His Majesty

Scripture: *"O Lord, our Lord, how majestic is Your name in all the earth!"* — Psalm 8:1
Revelation:
Worship unveils the majesty of God — His excellence and beauty made known through praise.
Declaration:
You are majestic, Lord! My worship proclaims Your greatness in all the earth.

Day 288 – Worship That Humbles the Heart

Scripture: *"God resists the proud, but gives grace to the humble."* — James 4:6
Revelation:
True worship bows low. In humility, grace flows — for only the broken can fully adore.
Declaration:
I bow before You, Lord. Let humility be the fragrance of my worship.

Day 289 – Worship That Unites Generations

Scripture: *"One generation shall praise Your works to another."* — Psalm 145:4
Revelation:
Worship is generational — passed from fathers to children. Each generation adds new songs to the same God.
Declaration:
Let my worship inspire the next generation, Lord. May praise never cease in our lineage.

Day 290 – Worship That Heals the Soul

Scripture: *"He heals the brokenhearted and binds up their wounds."* — Psalm 147:3
Revelation:
Worship brings divine healing to wounded hearts. His presence mends what words cannot.
Declaration:
Heal me, Lord, as I worship. Let Your presence bind my soul in wholeness.

Day 291 – Worship That Becomes a Testimony

Scripture: *"He put a new song in my mouth — a hymn of praise to our God."* — Psalm 40:3
Revelation:
Every song sung in faith tells a story of redemption. Worship testifies to the God who saves.
Declaration:
You've given me a new song, Lord. Let my worship be my living testimony.

Day 292 – Worship That Waits on His Timing

Scripture: *"Those who wait upon the Lord shall renew their strength."* — Isaiah 40:31

Revelation:

Worship teaches patience. Waiting in adoration strengthens trust and deepens love.

Declaration:

I wait in worship, Lord. My strength is renewed as I rest in You.

Day 293 – Worship That Blesses His Name Continually

Scripture: *"I will bless the Lord at all times; His praise shall continually be in my mouth."* — Psalm 34:1

Revelation:

Perpetual praise transforms every season into worship. Blessing God becomes a lifestyle, not an occasion.

Declaration:

I bless You at all times, Lord. May Your praise never leave my lips.

Day 294 – Worship That Breaks the Alabaster Box

Scripture: *"She broke the jar and poured it on His head."* — Mark 14:3

Revelation:

Brokenness releases fragrance. Worship that costs us everything fills eternity with beauty.

Declaration:

I break my life before You, Lord. Let my worship pour out as sweet perfume.

Day 295 – Worship That Sanctifies the Heart's Motive

Scripture: *"Man looks at the outward appearance, but the Lord looks at the heart."* — 1 Samuel 16:7

Revelation:

God weighs the heart of worship. What matters most is motive — pure love, not performance.

Declaration:

Search my heart, Lord. Let my worship spring from sincerity and truth.

Day 296 – Worship That Sustains in the Night

Scripture: *"At midnight I rise to give You thanks."* — Psalm 119:62

Revelation:

Even in darkness, worship brings light. Midnight praise births morning joy.

Declaration:

In my midnight, I will worship You. Your praise will be my song in the night.

Day 297 – Worship That Celebrates His Faithfulness

Scripture: *"Great is Your faithfulness!"* — Lamentations 3:23

Revelation:

Every moment of worship recalls His unchanging nature. His faithfulness is the foundation of our song.

Declaration:

Faithful God, I worship You. My praise is anchored in Your unchanging truth.

Day 298 – Worship That Declares His Dominion

Scripture: *"Yours is the kingdom, the power, and the glory forever."* — Matthew 6:13

Revelation:

Worship affirms divine authority. Every declaration of praise enthrones God over all.

Declaration:

Yours is the kingdom, Lord! My worship exalts Your dominion forever.

Day 299 – Worship That Aligns with His Will

Scripture: *"Not my will, but Yours be done."* — Luke 22:42

Revelation:

Worship yields the will. Adoration leads to surrender, aligning our hearts with heaven's desire.

Declaration:

Not my will, Lord — Yours alone. Let my worship echo Your perfect plan.

Day 300 – Worship That Prepares for Glory Eternal

Scripture: *"They will see His face, and His name shall be on their foreheads."* — Revelation 22:4

Revelation:

Worship is the foretaste of eternity — the practice of seeing, knowing, and loving Him forever.

Declaration:

Lord, prepare me for eternal worship. Let every song on earth ready me for heaven's glory.

Month 11
Days 301–330

Day 301 – Worship That Dwells in the Secret Place

Scripture: *"He who dwells in the secret place of the Most High shall abide under the shadow of the Almighty."* — Psalm 91:1

Revelation:
Worship is found in the secret place, where intimacy births confidence. Hidden adoration reveals His covering power.

Declaration:
Lord, I choose the secret place. Let my worship draw me under the shadow of Your wings.

Day 302 – Worship That Brings Heaven Near

Scripture: *"Your kingdom come, Your will be done on earth as it is in heaven."* — Matthew 6:10

Revelation:
Every act of true worship aligns earth with heaven. It invites divine order, presence, and power to manifest here.

Declaration:
As I worship, Lord, let heaven touch earth. Establish Your kingdom through my praise.

Day 303 – Worship That Births Obedience

Scripture: *"To obey is better than sacrifice."* — 1 Samuel 15:22

Revelation:
Worship without obedience is hollow. True adoration responds to God's word with surrender and action.

Declaration:
Lord, let my worship express itself in obedience. May my actions sing louder than my words.

Day 304 – Worship That Draws Fire from Heaven

Scripture: *"Then fire came down from heaven and consumed the burnt offering."* — 2 Chronicles 7:1
Revelation:
When worship pleases God, His fire falls. Heaven answers the sincere sacrifice of a worshipper's heart.
Declaration:
Send Your fire, Lord. Let my worship ignite heaven's response and consume all that is not of You.

Day 305 – Worship That Exalts His Word

Scripture: *"You have magnified Your word above all Your name."* — Psalm 138:2
Revelation:
Worship honors what God honors. When we exalt His Word, we glorify the essence of His nature.
Declaration:
I worship You, Lord, by treasuring Your Word. Let Scripture shape every song in my heart.

Day 306 – Worship That Reflects His Light

Scripture: *"Arise, shine, for your light has come!"* — Isaiah 60:1
Revelation:
Worshippers radiate divine light. When His glory rests on us, darkness must retreat.
Declaration:
Shine through me, Lord. Let my worship become a reflection of Your glorious light.

Day 307 – Worship That Declares His Righteousness

Scripture: *"The heavens proclaim His righteousness, and all the people see His glory."* — Psalm 97:6

Revelation:

Worship reveals the moral beauty of God — His righteousness displayed through praise.

Declaration:

Lord, I declare Your righteousness in my worship. Let Your glory be seen through my praise.

Day 308 – Worship That Finds Rest in His Presence

Scripture: *"My presence will go with you, and I will give you rest."* — Exodus 33:14

Revelation:

Worship brings rest to the soul. When we dwell in His presence, striving ceases and peace abides.

Declaration:

Lord, in Your presence I find rest. Let my worship quiet every storm within me.

Day 309 – Worship That Stands in Awe

Scripture: *"Let all the earth stand in awe of Him."* — Psalm 33:8

Revelation:

Awe is the posture of true worship. To stand amazed before His majesty is the highest form of praise.

Declaration:

I stand in awe of You, O Lord. May wonder fill my worship every day.

Day 310 – Worship That Reflects the Cross

Scripture: *"Worthy is the Lamb who was slain."* — Revelation 5:12

Revelation:

The cross is the center of all worship. Every song finds meaning at the feet of the slain Lamb.

Declaration:

Worthy are You, O Lamb of God. My worship bows before Your sacrifice and victory.

Day 311 – Worship That Invites His Beauty

Scripture: *"Worship the Lord in the beauty of holiness."* — Psalm 29:2

Revelation:

God's holiness is beautiful, not dreadful. Worship reveals the splendor of His perfection.

Declaration:

Lord, let the beauty of Your holiness fill my worship and transform my heart.

Day 312 – Worship That Brings Joy to Heaven

Scripture: *"There is joy in the presence of the angels of God over one sinner who repents."* — Luke 15:10

Revelation:

When hearts turn to God in worship, heaven rejoices. Our praise joins the celebration of redemption.

Declaration:

I worship You, Lord, with joy that mirrors heaven's delight. My praise joins the angels' chorus.

Day 313 – Worship That Rebuilds Ruins

Scripture: *"They shall raise up the former desolations."* — Isaiah 61:4

Revelation:

Worship restores what was lost. In adoration, the ruins of the soul and society are rebuilt by His presence.

Declaration:

Let my worship rebuild, Lord. Restore what was broken through the power of Your presence.

Day 314 – Worship That Sees Beyond the Veil

Scripture: *"The veil was torn in two."* — Matthew 27:51

Revelation:

The veil is gone — worship now enters unhindered. We behold His glory face to face through Christ.

Declaration:

I worship beyond the veil, Lord. I come boldly into Your holy presence.

Day 315 – Worship That Strengthens Faith

Scripture: *"Abraham did not waver through unbelief but gave glory to God."* — Romans 4:20

Revelation:

Worship reinforces faith. Glorifying God even in delay releases divine assurance.

Declaration:

Lord, I glorify You in faith. My worship declares that Your promise is sure.

Day 316 – Worship That Hosts His Glory in Simplicity

Scripture: *"In quietness and trust is your strength."* — Isaiah 30:15

Revelation:
Worship doesn't always roar — sometimes it whispers. Simplicity and trust invite profound glory.
Declaration:
Teach me to worship in quietness, Lord. Let still adoration host Your presence deeply.

Day 317 – Worship That Declares His Mercy

Scripture: *"His mercy endures forever."* — 2 Chronicles 20:21
Revelation:
Mercy is the anthem of heaven. Worship magnifies the compassion of a God who never gives up.
Declaration:
Your mercy endures forever, Lord. My worship celebrates Your unfailing love.

Day 318 – Worship That Turns Mourning to Dancing

Scripture: *"You turned my mourning into dancing."* — Psalm 30:11
Revelation:
Worship transforms sorrow into joy. The presence of God changes lament into celebration.
Declaration:
Turn my mourning to dancing, Lord. I worship You through every season of my soul.

Day 319 – Worship That Renews the Mind

Scripture: *"Be transformed by the renewing of your mind."* — Romans 12:2
Revelation:
Worship reorients our thinking. In His presence, our thoughts align with truth and beauty.

Declaration:
Renew my mind, Lord. Let my worship reshape the way I see You and the world.

Day 320 – Worship That Awakens Gratitude

Scripture: *"Enter His gates with thanksgiving and His courts with praise."* — Psalm 100:4
Revelation:
Gratitude is the gateway to worship. A thankful heart becomes a temple for His presence.
Declaration:
Thank You, Lord. My gratitude opens the gates for true worship.

Day 321 – Worship That Anchors the Soul

Scripture: *"We have this hope as an anchor for the soul."* — Hebrews 6:19
Revelation:
Worship steadies the drifting heart. In praising God's constancy, we find inner stability.
Declaration:
Anchor my soul, Lord, in worship and trust. My praise holds fast to Your unchanging truth.

Day 322 – Worship That Welcomes His Voice

Scripture: *"My sheep hear My voice."* — John 10:27
Revelation:
In worship, God speaks. His voice becomes clearer as hearts draw near in adoration.
Declaration:
Speak, Lord, for I am listening. Let my worship tune my heart to Your voice.

Day 323 – Worship That Restores Identity

Scripture: *"You are a chosen generation, a royal priesthood."* — 1 Peter 2:9

Revelation:

Worship reminds us who we are — priests called to offer spiritual sacrifices pleasing to God.

Declaration:

I am Yours, Lord — a worshipper set apart for Your glory.

Day 324 – Worship That Confounds the Proud

Scripture: *"God chose the foolish things to shame the wise."* — 1 Corinthians 1:27

Revelation:

Worship confuses worldly wisdom. Simple songs of faith carry heaven's authority.

Declaration:

Lord, use my worship to reveal Your power and humble the proud.

Day 325 – Worship That Overflows in Giving

Scripture: *"They first gave themselves to the Lord."* — 2 Corinthians 8:5

Revelation:

Generosity is worship in action. When we give ourselves, we mirror God's own heart.

Declaration:

Lord, I give myself completely to You. Let my worship overflow in generosity.

Day 326 – Worship That Exalts His Name Among Nations

Scripture: *"Be exalted, O God, above the heavens; let Your glory be over all the earth."* — Psalm 57:11

Revelation:

Worship has no borders. It's heaven's sound echoing across the nations.

Declaration:

Be exalted, Lord, in every land. Let my worship join the global anthem of Your glory.

Day 327 – Worship That Keeps the Heart Soft

Scripture: *"Today, if you hear His voice, do not harden your hearts."* — Hebrews 3:15

Revelation:

Worship tenderizes the heart. It keeps us responsive and pliable before God's touch.

Declaration:

Keep my heart soft, Lord. Let worship keep me sensitive to Your Spirit.

Day 328 – Worship That Rises Above Circumstances

Scripture: *"Though the fig tree does not bud… yet I will rejoice in the Lord."* — Habakkuk 3:17–18

Revelation:

Worship is not dependent on outcomes. It's the choice to praise God despite lack or loss.

Declaration:

Even when nothing blooms, I will worship You, Lord. You alone are my joy.

Day 329 – Worship That Anticipates His Return

Scripture: *"The Spirit and the Bride say, 'Come.'"* — Revelation 22:17

Revelation:

Every act of worship carries a longing cry — *Come, Lord Jesus.* Worship prepares the Bride for the Bridegroom.

Declaration:

Come, Lord Jesus. Let my worship echo the longing of heaven and earth.

Day 330 – Worship That Sees His Face

Scripture: *"When You said, 'Seek My face,' my heart said, 'Your face, Lord, I will seek.'"* — Psalm 27:8

Revelation:

The ultimate goal of worship is encounter — to see His face and be changed by His glory.

Declaration:

Your face, Lord, I seek. Let my worship lead me into the beauty of Your presence forever.

Month 12
Days 331–365

"The Eternal Song: Worship that Never Ends"

Day 331 – Worship That Echoes Eternity

Scripture: *"Holy, holy, holy is the Lord God Almighty, who was and is and is to come."* — Revelation 4:8

Revelation:

True worship carries the eternal sound — unending, unchanging, and unceasing. It joins heaven's timeless anthem.

Declaration:

Holy, holy, holy are You, Lord! Let my worship join the everlasting song of heaven.

Day 332 – Worship That Thrills the Heart of God

Scripture: *"The Father seeks those who will worship Him in spirit and truth."* — John 4:23

Revelation:

Worship is not man's search for God — it is God's search for worshippers. Nothing delights Him more than a heart fully His.

Declaration:

Father, I long to be found by You in worship. Let my spirit and truth bring joy to Your heart.

Day 333 – Worship That Rises as Incense

Scripture: *"Let my prayer be set before You as incense."* — Psalm 141:2

Revelation:

Worship ascends like sweet fragrance. Heaven receives it, and God inhales the aroma of love and surrender.

Declaration:
Lord, let my worship rise before You as incense — pure, pleasing, and continual.

Day 334 – Worship That Reigns in Silence

Scripture: *"Be still, and know that I am God."* — Psalm 46:10
Revelation:
Sometimes worship speaks loudest in silence. In stillness, our spirits bow, and heaven's peace floods our hearts.
Declaration:
In the quiet, I worship You, Lord. Your presence fills the silence with glory.

Day 335 – Worship That Mirrors Heaven's Order

Scripture: *"Let all things be done decently and in order."* — 1 Corinthians 14:40
Revelation:
Worship reflects heaven's order — unity, reverence, and alignment under divine authority.
Declaration:
Lord, align my worship with heaven's harmony. Let every note and act reflect Your order and peace.

Day 336 – Worship That Stirs the Spirit

Scripture: *"Stir up the gift of God which is in you."* — 2 Timothy 1:6
Revelation:
Worship fans the flame of the Spirit within. When we adore Him, His fire burns brighter in us.
Declaration:
Spirit of God, stir my heart through worship. Keep my passion for You alive and blazing.

Day 337 – Worship That Sees His Throne

Scripture: *"I saw the Lord sitting on a throne, high and lifted up."* — Isaiah 6:1

Revelation:

In worship, our eyes are lifted from earth to eternity. We behold the King in His beauty and majesty.

Declaration:

Lift my gaze, Lord. Let my worship behold Your throne and magnify Your reign.

Day 338 – Worship That Sanctifies the Moment

Scripture: *"Where two or three are gathered in My name, there am I in the midst of them."* — Matthew 18:20

Revelation:

Worship transforms ordinary moments into holy ground. His presence sanctifies time and place.

Declaration:

Be among us, Lord. Make every gathering holy through our worship.

Day 339 – Worship That Breathes His Life

Scripture: *"He breathed on them and said, 'Receive the Holy Spirit.'"* — John 20:22

Revelation:

When we worship, we inhale His presence and exhale His life. Worship is divine respiration.

Declaration:

Breathe on me, Lord. Let my worship carry the breath of Your Spirit.

Day 340 – Worship That Celebrates His Nearness

Scripture: *"The Lord is near to all who call on Him."* — Psalm 145:18

Revelation:

Worship isn't reaching far for God — it's responding to His nearness. He dwells with the adoring heart.

Declaration:

You are near, Lord. I worship You for being closer than my breath.

Day 341 – Worship That Magnifies His Majesty

Scripture: *"O magnify the Lord with me, and let us exalt His name together."* — Psalm 34:3

Revelation:

Worship enlarges our view of God. The more we magnify Him, the smaller our worries become.

Declaration:

I magnify You, O Lord! Be exalted above everything in my life.

Day 342 – Worship That Is Rooted in Humility

Scripture: *"God resists the proud, but gives grace to the humble."* — James 4:6

Revelation:

True worship bows low. Humility creates the platform for God's presence to rest.

Declaration:

I bow before You, Lord. Let humility be the fragrance of my worship.

Day 343 – Worship That Transcends Words

Scripture: *"Likewise the Spirit helps us… with groanings which cannot be uttered."* — Romans 8:26

Revelation:

Some worship goes beyond language — tears, sighs, and silence speak when words cannot.

Declaration:

Spirit of God, interpret my unspoken worship. Let my heart's cry reach Your throne.

Day 344 – Worship That Overflows in Compassion

Scripture: *"Be merciful, just as your Father is merciful."* — Luke 6:36

Revelation:

Worship transforms us to mirror His nature. The more we adore Him, the more His compassion flows through us.

Declaration:

Make my life an expression of Your mercy, Lord. Let worship make me more like You.

Day 345 – Worship That Celebrates the Blood

Scripture: *"We have boldness to enter the Holiest by the blood of Jesus."* — Hebrews 10:19

Revelation:

Worship stands on holy ground because of the blood. The Lamb's sacrifice grants us full access to His glory.

Declaration:

Thank You, Jesus, for the blood. I worship You for the doorway it opened into Your presence.

Day 346 – Worship That Anticipates Glory

Scripture: *"The glory of the Lord shall be revealed."* — Isaiah 40:5

Revelation:

Worship stirs expectation for greater revelation. Glory always follows hunger and holy anticipation.

Declaration:

Reveal Your glory, Lord. I worship in faith, expecting Your presence to fill the earth.

Day 347 – Worship That Rests in Wonder

Scripture: *"Great is the Lord, and greatly to be praised; His greatness is unsearchable."* — Psalm 145:3

Revelation:

Worship thrives in mystery. Wonder fuels adoration when words are not enough to describe His greatness.

Declaration:

You are beyond comprehension, Lord. I rest in the wonder of who You are.

Day 348 – Worship That Declares His Timelessness

Scripture: *"From everlasting to everlasting, You are God."* — Psalm 90:2

Revelation:

Worship anchors us in eternity. God was, is, and will forever be — our praise is the echo of forever.

Declaration:

From age to age, You are God! My worship joins the eternal praise of the ages.

Day 349 – Worship That Resounds in Creation

Scripture: *"The heavens declare the glory of God."* — Psalm 19:1

Revelation:

All creation worships. The stars, the seas, the mountains — each resounds with divine glory.

Declaration:

Lord, let my worship harmonize with creation's song of praise to You.

Day 350 – Worship That Carries Holy Fear

Scripture: *"Serve the Lord with fear, and rejoice with trembling."* — Psalm 2:11

Revelation:

Holy fear is not terror but reverent awe. It gives worship its depth and sincerity.

Declaration:

Lord, teach me the fear of Your name. Let reverence fill my worship.

Day 351 – Worship That Abides Forever

Scripture: *"His praise shall continually be in my mouth."* — Psalm 34:1

Revelation:

Worship never ends. In heaven, praise is the eternal language of love.

Declaration:

Lord, let my worship never cease. May praise flow through every breath I take.

Day 352 – Worship That Unites the Bride

Scripture: *"That they may be one, just as We are one."* — John 17:22

Revelation:

Worship unites the Body of Christ. One heart, one voice, one Bride preparing for one King.

Declaration:

Unite us, Lord, in worship. Let Your glory knit Your Bride together in perfect love.

Day 353 – Worship That Flows from the Throne

Scripture: *"A river of the water of life flowed from the throne of God and of the Lamb."* — Revelation 22:1

Revelation:

Worship flows like a river from His throne — life-giving, cleansing, and endless.

Declaration:

Let Your river flow through my worship, Lord. Refresh and renew me in Your presence.

Day 354 – Worship That is Crowned with Glory

Scripture: *"You crown the year with Your goodness."* — Psalm 65:11

Revelation:

God crowns every worshipper with His goodness. The one who exalts Him receives the radiance of His favor.

Declaration:

Crown this year, Lord, with Your glory. Let worship mark its every day.

Day 355 – Worship That Awakens Eternity Within

Scripture: *"He has set eternity in their hearts."* — Ecclesiastes 3:11

Revelation:

When we worship, eternity awakens inside us — a divine reminder of our everlasting purpose.

Declaration:

Eternity beats in my heart as I worship You, Lord. I was made for Your forever presence.

Day 356 – Worship That Fills the Earth

Scripture: *"The earth will be filled with the knowledge of the glory of the Lord."* — Habakkuk 2:14

Revelation:

Worship is God's plan for the earth. One day, every corner will resound with His glory.

Declaration:

Let Your glory fill the earth, Lord. Use my worship to be part of that sound.

Day 357 – Worship That Sings the New Song

Scripture: *"Sing to the Lord a new song."* — Psalm 96:1

Revelation:

The Spirit always releases new expressions of praise. Every season deserves its own melody.

Declaration:

Lord, give me a new song for this new day. Let fresh worship rise from my heart.

Day 358 – Worship That Brings Heaven's Reign

Scripture: *"The Lord sits enthroned upon the praises of Israel."* — Psalm 22:3

Revelation:

Worship builds a throne for God on earth. His rule manifests where His people exalt Him.

Declaration:
Be enthroned upon my praise, Lord. Reign over every area of my life.

Day 359 – Worship That Never Forgets His Benefits

Scripture: *"Bless the Lord, O my soul, and forget not all His benefits."* — Psalm 103:2
Revelation:
Remembrance fuels worship. Gratitude recalls His goodness and magnifies His faithfulness.
Declaration:
I bless You, Lord. I remember Your kindness and worship You with all my soul.

Day 360 – Worship That Ends in Glory

Scripture: *"To Him be glory in the church forever and ever."* — Ephesians 3:21
Revelation:
Worship doesn't end with us — it culminates in His eternal glory. All praise returns to its source.
Declaration:
To You be glory forever, Lord. Let all worship lead back to You alone.

Day 361 – Worship That Invites the Cloud of Glory

Scripture: *"The house was filled with a cloud, so that the priests could not stand to minister."* — 2 Chronicles 5:14
Revelation:
When worship reaches its peak, His glory descends tangibly. The divine cloud fills surrendered hearts.
Declaration:

Fill this temple, Lord. Let Your glory cloud rest upon my worship.

Day 362 – Worship That Shines Like the Bride

Scripture: *"His Bride has made herself ready."* — Revelation 19:7
Revelation:
Worship prepares the Bride for the wedding feast. Adoration adorns her in purity and light.
Declaration:
Lord, make me ready through worship. Clothe me in Your glory as Your Bride.

Day 363 – Worship That Joins the Multitude

Scripture: *"A great multitude… cried out, 'Salvation belongs to our God!'"* — Revelation 7:10
Revelation:
Worship connects us with the redeemed of all ages — one voice declaring His salvation.
Declaration:
I join the multitude, Lord! Salvation belongs to You alone.

Day 364 – Worship That Looks Upon His Face

Scripture: *"They shall see His face, and His name shall be on their foreheads."* — Revelation 22:4
Revelation:
The end of worship is encounter — to gaze upon the face of Love forever.
Declaration:

Your face I long to see, Lord. Let my worship lead me home to You.

Day 365 – Worship That Never Ends

Scripture: *"To Him who sits on the throne and to the Lamb be blessing and honor and glory and power forever and ever."* — Revelation 5:13

Revelation:

The eternal destiny of every worshipper is unending praise. The song begun on earth continues in heaven.

Declaration:

Forever and ever, Lord, You are worthy! Let my worship echo through eternity — unending, unbroken, and forever Yours.

About the Author 'GERARD ASSEY'

Gerard Assey is a Graduate in Economics, a PGD in Management (HRD) and holds a Doctorate in Leadership. Gerard holds several International Qualifications in Sales, Debt Collection, Training & Teaching, and is a 'Fellow' of the prestigious 'Institute of Sales & Marketing Management'-UK, a Certified NLP Practitioner, a 'Certified Trainer', an 'Accredited Management Teacher-Behavioral Sciences', a 'Certified Competency Facilitator', a 'Certified Management Consultant'- (the International credentials of a professional management consultant, awarded in accordance with global standards of the ICMCI); and a Certification from the University of Michigan in 'Successful Negotiation: Essential Strategies and Skills'

He is also a Member of the 'National Association of Sales Professionals' backed with several years experience in varied industries, both in India and Overseas. He also holds an 'Etiquette Consultant' Certification from the USA (by Sue Fox, Author of Best Seller: 'Business Etiquette for Dummies'. She has trained some of the top celebrities' world over). He was also a recipient of a scholarship for extensive training in Japan on 'Corporate Management for India'.

Gerard Assey is 'Founder & Chief Corporate Trainer' of the Group: '**Citius, Altius, Fortius Unlimited**'- an organization that **celebrated 20 years of Glorious Service** in 2021, focusing on 3 Core Competencies:

People. Performance. Profit; in functional areas of Sales & Marketing, HR & Organizational Development, covering Recruitment, Training & Consultancy!

Having managed organizations with large Sales Forces in India & Overseas, his specialization cover extensive areas of Sales Training (All levels - Presentation, Negotiation, Key/ Strategic Accounts Management & Managerial Skills for all sectors), Bid Proposal/ Capture Planning/ Management Trainings, Retail Sales, Customer Service & Customer Retention Programs, Training for Prevention & Collection of Debt, Self & Personal Development Programs (Time Management, Teamwork & Team Building, Business Etiquette & Personal Grooming, Leadership & Managerial Skills, People Management Skills, Train-the-Trainer etc), including preparation of Custom-designed Business Manuals for Internal (HR, Induction, and Sales etc) & External use (Instruction, User Manuals).

Gerard has successfully conducted over 6490 Trainings & Workshops (as of Nov '25) all across India, Middle East, Africa, Europe & S.E. Asia. Besides public programs conducted regularly, both in India & Overseas, he has some of the top names as clients whom he services from Single Owners to large Public & Government undertakings, covering all sectors, for their in-house needs.

His website: www.CollectionSkills.com is the only one in this part of the world to be featured in the 'Collections & Credit Risk Magazine-USA' under 'Who's Who in Training' and ranks TOP, along with other websites listed below on most search engines.

Gerard is author of 209 Books already (Nov 2025), all the books being available on all online platforms and outlets as E-books and Paperbacks

A few of our business related books:

1. Bite-sized Bits on Commonsense Management
2. Heart to Heart on Life's Principles'
3. How to become a Successful Manager
4. The Sales Professionals' Master Workbook of S.Y.S.T.E.M.S
5. The Professional Business Email Etiquette Handbook & Guide
6. The Professional Business Video-Conferencing Etiquette Handbook & Guide
7. Professional Presentation Skills
8. Exceptional Customer Service
9. Professional Tele-Marketing Skills
10. Professional Debt Collection Skills
11. The G.R.E.A.T. Sales & Service Workbook
12. Sales Training Advantage for Results (*The Ultimate Sales Training Manual to enable you stand out as a S.T.A.R.*)
13. CEO Daily Planner & Organizer
14. The Sales Professionals' Master Daily Planner
15. The Professional Debt Collector's Master Daily Planner
16. My Daily Planner & Organizer
17. MY EMERGENCY INFORMATION RECORD (Family Emergency & Peace of Mind Planner)
18. The Ultimate Therapist & Counselors Planner and Organizer
19. Building an Ethical Workplace
20. Managing Relationships at Work
21. Managing Business Meetings Effectively
22. Effective Delegation Skills
23. Goal Setting for Success
24. B2B Selling by Email
25. Professional Business Etiquette & Grooming
26. Dining Etiquette & Table Manners
27. Effective Networking Skills
28. Grooming, Etiquette & Manners for Teens, Young Adults & Future Leaders
29. Inter-Personal Skills
30. Get Ready, Get Hired!
31. Selling in a Recession
32. Effective Receivables Management in an Economic Downturn!
33. Real Estate & Property Sales Training
34. Credit Sales & Accounts Receivable Management

35. Selling Skills for Real Estate & Property Advisors
36. Take G.R.E.A.T. C.A.R.E!
37. Spa, Salon & Health Club Selling Skills
38. Selling Travel, Holiday & MICE Services
39. Selling Skills for Spa's, Salons & Health Clubs
40. Retailing in Salons & Spas
41. Selling Holiday, Vacation, Tours & Packages
42. The Power of Sales Referrals
43. Selling Luxury
44. Technical Selling Skills
45. Financial Advisors Sales Training
46. Dealing with Burnout at Work Monopolize Your Markets
47. Selling to Affluent Customers
48. Growing up with Grace
49. Financial Selling Skills
50. *The Effective Manager's Guide: Key Skills to Thrive*
51. From Aspiring to Inspiring: A Guide for New Managers on the Rise
52. The Power of Focus
53. Selling with Integrity: Sell Like Jesus The Perfect Role Model!
54. 31 Habits of Champions: Your 31-Day Journey to Greatness
55. Rejecting Grasshopper Talk: From Grasshopper to Giant-Killer-*Defeating Giants Daily!*
56. Navigate the AI-Powered Future of Bid & Proposals: Up-Skill to Stay Relevant with Alternative Career Paths & Opportunities
57. Hiring Sales Winners
58. Present with Impact
59. Success Unlocked: *Breaking Free from Habits that Hold You Back*
60. Complaints to Cheers, Feedback to Gold: Mastering Complaints Management
61. Thriving Together: *Cultivating Diversity, Equity, and Inclusion*
62. Coaching Skills for Sales Managers
63. Soaring to Success in Business & Leadership: Swifter, Higher, Stronger!
64. From Classroom to Podium: A Student's Guide to Powerful Public Speaking & Presentation Skills
65. Developing Self-Discipline
66. The CEO's 31-Day Power Plan: Unlocking Success through Essential Traits

67. Credibility Matters
68. A Winning Attitude
69. Bid & Proposal Management Using AI
70. Sales Forecasting: A Practical & Proven Guide to Strategic Sales Forecasting
71. Elevate & Energize: *50 Dynamic & Fun Activities for Peak Workplace Morale*
72. 'Sales SOS! Sales on Fire! *30 Days to Conquer Chaos & the Nightmares of Success!'*
73. Mastering Sales Managerial Skills: *Building High-Performing Teams & Driving Exceptional Results*
74. Eagle-Eyed Leadership: Unleashing the Power of 31 Lessons from Eagles
75. The Ultimate Employee Training Guide: *Training Today, Leading Tomorrow*
76. Being More Accountable at Work
77. Creating a Culture of Continuous Improvement
78. Effective Questioning & Listening Skills
79. The Power of Value Selling
80. The Growth Mindset
81. Mastering Professional Help Desk Skills
82. The Power to Lead with Empathy
83. Being Prepared: The Key to Unlocking Success
84. Youthful Spark-Youth Energizers, Activities and Games-Igniting the Fun in Youth
85. Ignite your Motivation for Success
86. Elevate Your Executive Presence: *Your Roadmap to Executive Excellence*
87. Smart Decisions: *Mastering Problem Solving with Strategic Solutions for Business Success*
88. Strategic Planning: *Developing and Implementing Strategic Plans to Achieve Long-Term Business Goals*
89. The Power of Stay Interviews
90. Developing G.R.I.T.
91. Adaptability
92. Diagnosis- *A Key Skill for Leadership*
93. The Burnout-Proof Salesperson: *The Master Guide to Preventing Stress & Burnout*- Strategies for Thriving in Sales
94. Learning from Failure: *Keys to Success*
95. Customer Success Management
96. Overcoming the Killers of Motivation
97. The C-Suite Code: *Mastering Skills for Executive Excellence'*

98. Dealing with Difficult Customers
99. Unlocking Your Potential: Mastering the Top 20 Life Skills for a Brighter Future
100. Nurturing Tomorrow's Leaders: *Essential Soft Skills Every Child Must Learn*
101. Lively & Fun Party Games for Seniors & Elders
102. Role Playing for Sales Champions: From Practice to Performance
103. Fun and Exciting Party Games for Kids
104. Case Studies for Sales
105. Role-Playing for Unbeatable Customer Service
106. Case Studies in Customer Service
107. Case Studies in Winning Negotiations
108. Case Studies in Management & Leadership
109. Case Studies in Human Resources & Talent Management
110. CEO Success Blueprint: The Essential Toolkit for CEOs and C-Level Executives
111. The Salesperson's Self-Coaching Guide: *Master Your Own Self-Coaching Plan for Success*
112. Overcoming Procrastination: *Your Ultimate Guide to Stop Delaying and Start Living Your Best Life*
113. When True Colors Are Exposed: *The Journey to Unmasking Humanity*
114. Life-Changing Habits for Teens: Teen Success Blueprint for a Bright Future
115. Workplace Stress-Free: *Proven Strategies to Thrive at Work and Beyond*
116. Objection Overruled: *The Ultimate Guide to Turning 'No' into 'Yes'*
117. Building Strong Teams: *A Comprehensive Guide to Team Building*
118. Ethical & Moral Leadership in Business: *Eliminating Unethical Practices & Building a Culture of Trust & Integrity*
119. Rising Strong: Building Positive: High Self-Esteem for a Fulfilling Life-*A Practical Guide for Students, Employees, Leaders & Entrepreneurs*
120 The Cheerful Mindset: Cultivating a Joyful Outlook Everyday
121. Leading Through Crisis: Case Studies on Crisis Management

From the Ministry side, Gerard graduated in the very first batch of Charis Bible College-India & had for over 9 years served as a Part-time Faculty at Charis Bible College-Chennai (Andrew Wommack Ministries-Colorado, USA).
He also holds a Diploma in Worship (a subject closest to his heart) from the JSOW and is also a graduate of the Advanced Mentorship Program (AMP) and the Circle Of Ministerial Engagement (C.O.M.E.) of Prophet Jerome Fernando and a Spiritual Son of the Esteemed Prophet.
An accomplished author of several Secular & Christian Books, Gerard has been on the board of a few international organizations and boasts of being the SON of the MOST HIGH GOD: An ordinary guy following an extraordinary GOD!

...And some of his most recent Christian Books being:

1. A Bouquet of Praises for My KING
2. Christian Jokes for the Serious Religious' Folks!
3. Jesus Healed You!
4. Praise24Ever! (also in Tamil version)
5. The 5G Network of GOD
6. Building Faith over F.E.A.R- FACE EVERYTHING AND RISE with JESUS
7. Hebrew and Greek Praise and Worship Words
8. Godly Mothers' and Grandmothers' Bible Story time for Kids!
9. Miracles of Jesus in Pictures
10. Raise your Praise all 365 Days
11. Thanking GOD with an Attitude of Gratitude
12. Meditating on the Attributes of GOD
13. Puppet Scripts
14. Alcohol Ruins, JESUS Reforms, Renews & Restores!
15. Habakkuk 2:2 Christian Daily Journal, Planner & Organizer
16. ABC of GOD's Word for Handwriting Practice
17. Daily Bible Verse Handwriting Practice (Building Godly Character & Faith through Cursive Handwriting Practice!)
18. Guiding Light: Fun & Faith-Building Bible Activities for Children
19. Rejecting Grasshopper Talk: From Grasshopper to Giant-Killer-*Defeating Giants Daily!*
20. Teen Titans of Faith: *Building Courage, Determination & Christ-like-Esteem*
21. I AM Empowered: *Unleashing Divine Power with Positive*

Declarations

22. Be A Solution Provider-*From Passion to Purpose*: *A Biblical Guide to Being the Answer to the World!*
23. Miracles of JESUS
24. Parables of Jesus for a Meaningful Life!
25. A Grateful Heart: Importance of Sharing Testimonies of GOD's Grace
26. Melodies of Worship to JESUS: 31 Songs of Praise & Worship From My Heart to HIS!
27. I AM SO BLESSED!
28. My Daily Cup of Energizer
29. 31 Leadership Lessons *from* Jesus- *The Supreme Leader*
30. Peace Amidst Storms: A Biblical Guide to Conquering S.T.R.E.S.S.
31. Rise Above: 20 Biblical Eagle Lessons for Life's Triumphs
32. Godly Goal Setting: *The FAITHFUL Blueprint for a Purpose-Driven Life*
33. The Profound Attributes of our Mighty GOD: Understanding the 10S's of the Almighty
34. Worship Now, Worship Forever: *A Journey from Earthly Praise to Eternal Glory*
35. Unceasing Praise & Worship: *365 Days to Worship the King*
36. The ROAR Within: *Living with Purpose and Authority through the Power of the Holy Spirit*
37. From Potential to Purpose: Unlocking and Multiplying Your Talents & Gifts for Kingdom Impact
38. Songs from the Heart: *Worshipping GOD in Your Own Tune & Melody*
39. Awakening Praise & Worship: Hebrew & Greek Words to Raise Your Praise
40. Sing a NEW Song to the LORD Everyday: *Daily Devotions of Praise & Worship to Lift Your Heart & Glorify HIS Name*
41. *The* A.R.O.M.A. of True Worship: *Creating Worship That Delights God*
42. Becoming A Kingdom Champion: *Embracing God's Call for a Life of Purpose & Victory*
43. The Busy Businessman's Daily Devotional: 366 Crisp Truths to Start Your Day Strong
44. The Teacher's Heart: *Daily Devotions for Educators*
45. Anchored! *A 31-Day Devotional for Students Facing Life's Challenges*
46. Suddenly! Unlocking Unorthodox Breakthroughs through Unusual Worship

47. Overcoming Adversity: *Lessons from the Bible for Modern Challenges*
48. LORD, Don't do it without me
49. Kingdom Leadership: *Biblical Principles for Modern Leaders*
50. Heartprints of God- *Growing God's Way:* Daily Devotions for Kids to Shine Bright
51. Send Judah First: Let your Praises Go up First to See the Mighty Move of GOD
52. DIVINE MOMENTS: *Recognizing, Embracing, Preparing, and Walking into Life-Changing Encounters with God*
53. Be a Builder in the Kingdom: *The C.E.M.E.N.T. Guide to Creating a Lasting Legacy*
54. Unshakable: *Pillars of Godly Womanhood* (Pillars of Faith That Changed History)
55. Lead Like a Shepherd: *14 Essential Traits for Pastoral Excellence*
56. The Worship Leader's Arsenal: *Powerful Exhortations to Ignite Thanksgiving, Praise & Worship*
57. Women of UnShakable Faith: *31-Day Devotional for Strength, Purpose & Influence*
58. Called to Teach: *A Complete 10-Week Training Guide for Impactful VBS Teachers*
59. Strumming for the KING: Cowboy Songs of Faith & Fire
60. The Ultimate Youth Camp Playbook: *50 Bible-Centered Indoor Games to Engage, Equip, and Empower Teens*
61. Glad in HIS Presence: *David's Revelation of GOD's Love & Mercy*
62. The Spirit Behind the Sound: *52 Devotionals for Worship Teams*
63. THE COWBOY'S COMPASS: *Riding the Trail of Faith with Grit & Grace*
64. Worship as My Weapon: *Living Victoriously through the Power of Praise*
65. A Worshipper Always Wins*: Living a Life of Victorious Worship*
66. Worship That Leads to the Throne: *Practical Strategies for Worship Leaders to Inspire Their Team & Usher People into God's Presence*
67. Worship as Warfare: *Conquering through the Sound of Surrender*
68. Watchmen on the Walls: *A 31-Day Devotional for Worship Teams*

69. KINGDOM BUSINESS: *52 Biblical Principles for GODLY Leadership & Wise Decisions*
70. From Evening to Morning: *Rediscovering GOD's Sacred Hours*
71. Waves of Glory: *Worship through Dance, Flags, Staff & Sound*
72. WORSHIP TEAM BUILDER: *Guiding Your Team from Formation to Fruitfulness*
73. The Worship Leader's Master Training Manual
74. Skits for the King: Children's Plays for Every Church Occasion
75. Unbreakable: Building Strong Marriages and Families God's Way *(From Vows to Victory)*
76. Songs for my King: *A 31-Day Journey of Praise*
77. Building Powerful Children: *Raising a Generation That Will Shape the Future for God*
78. Character Before Chords: *The Heart of the True Worshipper*
79. 365 Days Before His Throne: A Worshipper's Daily Declarations

Besides regularly contributing to business & trade journals, including international ones such as the 'Creative Training Techniques' and the 'Sales News' of the U.S.A, He is also a member of several prestigious bodies & trade associations, having participated in many Conferences & Workshops in India & Overseas.

Prior to his last assignment of leading & managing a large MNC as head, Gerard had a 3-year stint in the Middle East as a Consultant with a leading British Consultancy Firm.

As the past 'Official Country Representative' for the International Business Award- 'THE STEVIES'-(the business world's own Oscar) for about 4 years- he ensured a few Indian companies that qualify for the same every year!

Gerard can be contacted at:
Email: training@Sales-Training.in,training@CollectionSkills.com
Websites:
www.Sales-Training.in
www.EtiquetteWorks.in
www.CollectionSkills.com
www.RetailSalesTraining.in
www.SalesTrainingIndia.com
www.ManualPreparation.com
www.TrainingWithPuppets.com
www.FirstContactAcademy.com
www.SalesAndMarketingRecruiter.com

www.ingramcontent.com/pod-product-compliance
Ingram Content Group UK Ltd.
Pitfield, Milton Keynes, MK11 3LW, UK
UKHW021340190726
13845UKWH00027B/640

9 788199 500112